LANCASTER AND LANCASTER COUNTY

LANCASTER AND LANCASTER COUNTY

A Traveler's Guide to Pennsylvania Dutch Country

Anthony D. Fredericks

THE COUNTRYMAN PRESS
WOODSTOCK, VERMONT

Interior photographs by the author unless otherwise specified
Map by Michael Borop, siteatlas.com, © The Countryman Press
Book design by S. E. Livingston
Composition by Chelsea Cloeter

Published by The Countryman Press,
P.O. Box 748, Woodstock, VT 05091

Distributed by W. W. Norton & Company, Inc.,
500 Fifth Avenue, New York, NY 10110

Printed in the United States of America

10 9 8 7 6 5 4 3 2 1

Lancaster and Lancaster County
ISBN 978-1-58157-214-8

TO THE MEMORY OF MICHAEL AREZZI— TRAVELER, BON VIVANT, FAMILY MAN, AND FRIEND

The Amish Village

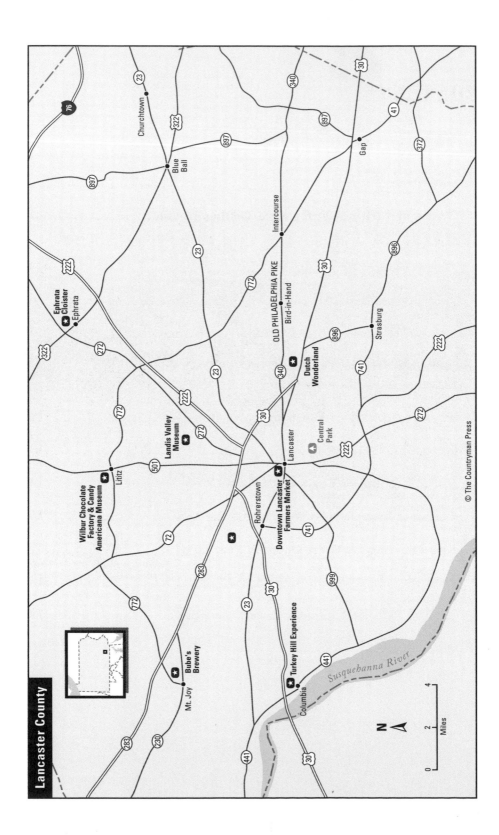

Lancaster County

Churchtown

Blue Ball

Intercourse

Ephrata Cloister
● Ephrata

OLD PHILADELPHIA PIKE

Bird-in-Hand

Gap

Strasburg

Dutch Wonderland

Landis Valley Museum

Lancaster

Central Park

Wilbur Chocolate Factory & Candy Americana Museum

Lititz

Downtown Lancaster Farmers Market

Rohrerstown

Mt. Joy

Bube's Brewery

Turkey Hill Experience

Columbia

Susquehanna River

N

Miles

0   2   4

© The Countryman Press

CONTENTS

Visit an Amish farm.

INTRODUCTION

More than 11 million visitors travel to Lancaster County every year. They arrive from all 50 states and many foreign countries. They come to savor a slice of molasses-rich shoo-fly pie; tour the quaint towns of Bird-in-Hand, Intercourse, and Paradise; travel on a historic steam locomotive past rolling green farmlands; ride authentic Amish buggies through the scenic countryside; and shop the farmer's markets and unique stores sprinkled along the county's thoroughfares.

For many, Lancaster and Lancaster County, Pennsylvania, is the quintessential vacation destination—the ultimate "Pennsylvania Dutch" experience. It's a return to simpler times, long before the onset of golden-arched restaurants, supersonic travel, or Facebook. This is time slowed down—a pace of life considerably more pleasant and less demanding. It's strolling, rather than dashing; it's gazing, rather than glimpsing; and it's conversation, rather than e-mails.

The origins of the Pennsylvania Dutch go back to the 17th and 18th centuries when immigrants from southwestern Germany, Switzerland, and Alsace settled in Pennsylvania—principally in the southern and eastern regions of the state. (Interestingly, the word *Dutch* is frequently believed to be a corruption of the word for "German" or *Deutsch*. In fact, *Dutch* is a legitimate term originally used by the English to identify those people who lived along the Rhine River.) They were attracted here by William Penn's embrace of religious freedom and the availability of agriculturally rich land. Historically, these people spoke the dialect of German known as Pennsylvania Dutch or Pennsylvania German. This dialect retains some of its Germanic precepts, but is uniquely distinctive in both meter and cadence. Even today, if you listen closely, you can still hear echoes of this language in some of the commercial enterprises you visit throughout Lancaster County.

> **FAST FACT:** The tourist economy of Lancaster County generates nearly $1.8 billion every year.

For it is here that you can 1) roll past 200-year-old Amish farms plowed

Roadside stands abound with fresh produce.

by plodding horses and young boys in straw hats, 2) walk beside the rolling Susquehanna River in a "slice out of time" colonial town, 3) taste some authentic homemade root beer (absolutely no preservatives) at a roadside stand, 4) visit the 19th-century mansion of Pennsylvania's only president, 5) stand in a small hotel that was a flashpoint for the American Civil War, 6) drive across a classic Pennsylvania covered bridge, 7) visit the home of a Revolutionary War hero, or (best yet) 8) just take some time to chill. Lancaster County is one of those magical places in Pennsylvania Dutch country that will recharge your batteries and revitalize you as few places can—it's a treat for the senses and an oasis for the psyche. In so many ways, it's what vacations are all about—rest, recreation, and rejuvenation.

I'd like to invite you to come along on an incredible visit—one that will energize and refresh as well as educate and inspire. I'd like to share some incredible sights and equally incredible people who made this part of the country so rich in heritage, culture, and visual riches. Lancaster and Lancaster County await your discovery. So come on along—the journey's about to begin.

The experiences that await you in Pennsylvania Dutch Country—specifically, Lancaster and Lancaster County—are unparalleled and exceptional. Like an artist's palette, there is a rich mix of vibrant colors, a panoply of educational treats and an abundance of down-home friendliness here. Lancaster County is like visiting a cruise ship smorgasbord table piled high with epicurean delights and gastronomical delicacies. Which ones to choose, which ones to sample? For the first-time visitor, selecting the items to fill your vacation plate will indeed be a challenge of epic proportions. The history, culture, and people of the county beckon at every turn of the road or fold of the map. This is a piece of Americana that begs for multiple visits and sojourns just so you can sample all the wares and experience all the delights.

As you ponder your decisions, I'd like to offer a few words of advice—particularly if this is your first visit into Lancaster County. These suggestions come from someone who has lived next door to Lancaster County for more than a quarter-century; someone who has made countless journeys across this landscape for exotic culinary delights, panoramic visual pleasures, dramatic historical sites, and incredible lifetime memories . . . and continues to do so.

An Amish buggy at the "service station"

Every effort has been made to provide you with the most accurate information about each and every site in this book. Addresses, phone numbers, and websites have been checked to ensure they are current and accurate (as of this writing). However, places change—new owners take over, venues are updated and renovated, philosophies change and various economic challenges frequently rear their ugly heads. What I may write in this book today and what may be in effect when you visit two or three years hence may be quite different. It's always prudent to check in advance (call or check the website) to make sure your plans aren't derailed by unforeseen economic forces or cruel business realities.

Remember, you're on vacation. This is not the time to do the "same old, same old." Try some new things, visit some new places, and sample some new foods. Don't stay in the same chain hotel that's down the street in your hometown and don't eat the same food in the same chain restaurant that's in the mall around the corner from where you live. This is vacation time—a time to sample the different, try the unusual, and experience what you've never experienced before. Stop in at an Irish pub just because you've never sampled Irish ale before. Buy a jar of chow-chow at a farmer's roadside stand just because . . . well, just because the name sounds funny. Stop by Lancaster's Central Market just because you've never been in a 275-year-old grocery store. Learn how pretzels are made, then make your own. Visit an Underground Railroad museum or a former president's house just because you'd like to make your high-school history lessons come alive. Or ride a hot-air balloon over the Lancaster County countryside. Again, this is your vacation—try something new. Be different! Be daring! Be bold!

This is a wonderful opportunity to immerse yourself in the culture of Lancaster County. Many people journey here to see and experience the Amish way of life—where thousands still live a centuries-old "plain" lifestyle. While in Lancaster County you'll be able to step back in time to enjoy their slower, more peaceful pace—one where the horse and buggy remains a primary form of transportation, where windmills dot the landscape, and where family farms that have been passed down through multiple generations still produce crops as diverse as tobacco, corn, and alfalfa.

You'll also be able to take authentic buggy rides past Amish farms, visit Amish homes, eat Amish food, and purchase Amish quilts to take home. Indeed, there is any number of commercial enterprises eager to provide you with a sampling of Amish life. But I'd like to suggest that, for a truer experience, you should escape some of the robust commercial enterprises and head off the beaten track (off PA-

Lancaster Central Market, your 275-year-old supermarket

FAST FACT: Lancaster County is home to the oldest Amish community in the United States.

340) to discover some Amish culture along the numerous backroads and byways of Lancaster County.

Stop at a roadside stand and purchase some fresh vegetables or homemade shoo-fly pie. Strike up a conversation with the owner of a quilt store on a side road and ask about the work and skill she puts into her creations. Drive some of the backroads north or south of Lancaster past Amish farms (no electric or phone lines, plain and simple houses) and watch young girls tending to household chores or boys tilling a tobacco field. Walk around a one-room schoolhouse and admire its simplicity. Away from some of the more glitzy ventures, you'll truly appreciate and understand Amish values and culture. But please don't be invasive—don't knock on their doors, interrupt their work, peek in windows, or take photographs.

Although many visitors come to Lancaster County in the summer months,

Farming is a way of life in Lancaster County.

you will discover that this region is ripe for exploration all year long. If possible, plan a visit for early spring when flowers are blooming and farm work begins in earnest. Opt for an autumn visit when farm stands are filled with all sorts of goodies and the stores are considerably less crowded. Lancaster County is one of those places that values visitors all through the year. There's always plenty to see and do no matter what season you decide to visit. In the "off" season the pace is slower, the sites less crowded and the journey less hectic. Indeed, there is magic here no matter what the time of year.

You will discover that a single visit to Lancaster County is not enough (approximately two-thirds of all visitors to Lancaster County will visit again, according to the Lancaster County Pennsylvania Visitor Center). There is simply too much to do and see. Although my wife and I have lived next to Lancaster County for more than 25 years, we still have many places we want to visit, new restaurants we want to sample, and hordes of off-road sights we want to see. For us, Lancaster County is our "vacation next door." We love nothing better than to toss a picnic basket in the back of the car and set out to discover a historical site in a remote corner of the county, a majestic overlook with hundred-mile views in every direction, a new roadside stand to get some farm-fresh vegetables, or an antique dealer with that one-of-a-kind knickknack perfect for the living room table.

To truly experience all that Lancaster has to offer, you'll need to return several times. Each new visit and each new journey will reveal a host of surprises and a cornucopia of delights. This is a county that never fails to satisfy and impress. Take it from a frequent wanderer—your visit (or visits) to Lancaster County will definitely energize and refresh, as well as educate and inspire.

Ready? Let's go!

Travel to Lancaster County and enjoy the vacation of a lifetime!

1 Transportation
GETTING HERE, GETTING AROUND

The history of transportation in Lancaster County is rooted in its Native American past—specifically the foot paths Native Americans used to travel across this rich and varied landscape. Most of the foot travel through forests and fields was for the purpose of trade—the exchange of goods and food between and among the scattered and often isolated villages.

The primary village (in what is now Lancaster County) was Conestoga—a central trading outpost located about 4 miles southwest of the present-day borough of Millersville. Conestoga (meaning *at the place of the immersed pole*) was a critical center of trade and foot traffic from approximately 1690 to 1740. Not only was the village a central point for Native Americans, it was also a popular trade center for settlers, explorers and the early pioneers to this region shortly after the territory was opened up by William Penn.

Conestoga's importance lay in the fact that it was at the convergence of six or seven foot paths, each of which led in a different direction throughout present-day Pennsylvania. One of the primary foot paths into and out of Conestoga was the Great Minquas Path—a 17th-century trade route that arched eastward through vast wooded lands and across numerous tributaries toward the Schuylkill River and the European settlements of Philadelphia and Chester. This 80-mile trail was so significant that Dutch, English, and Swedish settlers fought over it continuously for many years. That this route was an important transportation artery is reflected in the fact that long segments of today's US-222 and PA-741 follow the same lines in Lancaster County as did the original Great Minquas Path (also known as the Great Trail).

Many first-time visitors to Lancaster County inquire about the viability of the Susquehanna River as a transportation artery. Indeed, one might imagine

The Susquehanna River forms the western boundary of Lancaster County.

that this 464-mile river, which forms the western boundary of Lancaster County, would be a logical and natural transportation artery.

Unfortunately, the Susquehanna is noted for a large number of rocks, hidden rapids, and very shallow expanses. As such, it now has the distinction of being the longest non-navigable river in the United States (it is also the 16th-largest river in the U.S.). Commercial boat travel up and down the Susquehanna was not only impractical, it was impossible.

The first railroad to pass through Lancaster County was the Philadelphia and Columbia Railroad (in 1834), which connected the city of Lancaster with the Susquehanna River town of Columbia. Soon after in 1836, the Harrisburg, Portsmouth, Mount Joy and Lancaster Railroad constructed a connecting line from Mount Joy to Dillersville. This was followed by the Strasburg Railroad, which was completed in 1837. The Strasburg line is still in operation today as a tourist railroad (we'll visit it later in this book) and is one of Lancaster County's most popular visitor attractions.

Today's travelers to Lancaster County can come and go via several transportation options—air, rail, bus, or car. Although mass transportation outside the city limits of Lancaster is somewhat limited (with the exception of the always popular and always well-traveled Pennsylvania Turnpike, I-76), there are still many ways of getting around. The best is by car—a sprinkling of delightful small towns, the rich and awe-inspiring vistas, the quaint and delightfully rural back roads, and the singularly unique culture of Lancaster County almost demands the use of a car. Yet however you travel and wherever you go throughout the county, you will be rewarded with an array of visual delights—much as the early pioneers were as they traipsed along well-worn foot paths from village to village.

> **F**AST FACT: The Susquehanna River drains an area of 27,500 square miles—nearly one-half of the land area of Pennsylvania.

A Strasburg Rail Road historic steam locomotive.

GETTING TO LANCASTER COUNTY

Although Lancaster and Lancaster County may be considered rural and remote by many, there is still a wide diversity of transportation options available for visitors. Getting here and getting around is remarkably easy. Consider the following options.

BY AIR

There are three primary airports. They are listed here in order of proximity to Lancaster.

Harrisburg International Airport (888-235-9442; www.flyhia.com; 1 Terminal Drive #300, Middletown, PA 17057). Harrisburg International Airport (MDT) is a mere 32 miles from downtown Lancaster. It is a very easy airport to get in and out of (I use it almost exclusively when I travel). It is served by a number of carriers including Air Canada, Allegiant, Delta Air Lines, Frontier Airlines, United Airlines, and American/USAirways. These airlines provide daily, nonstop service to 14 destinations, along with one-stop connections to numerous cities throughout the world.

Baltimore Washington International Airport (800-435-9294; www.bwiairport .com; P.O. Box 8766, BWI Airport, MD 21240). Baltimore Washington Inter-

Harrisburg International Airport (HIA)

national Airport (BWI) lies 90 miles south of downtown Lancaster. The drive from BWI to Lancaster is relatively easy—except if you arrive during rush hour, during which your journey around Baltimore (on I-695) will be much slower than you would

FAST FACT: In 2009, *Forbes* named Lancaster County one of the Ten Best American Towns to Visit by Car.

like. Every major carrier flies in and out of BWI, and you can get non-stop flights from all major U.S. cities into Baltimore.

Philadelphia International Airport (215-937-6937; www.phl.org; 8800 Essington Ave Philadelphia, PA 19153). Philadelphia International Airport (PHL) is the largest airport in the region. It is situated approximately 92 miles east of Lancaster if you use the Pennsylvania Turnpike (I-76) for most of your journey. Travel in and around the airport is frequently congested and confusing and the infamous Schuylkill Expressway, particularly during rush hour, can slow you down considerably. PHL is serviced by all major (and several minor) airlines.

AIRPORT GROUND TRANSPORTATION

The airport websites provide valuable information on ground transportation and security.

Harrisburg International Airport. The airport's website (http://flyhia.com/ground_transportation) has complete information about a wide variety of ground transportation options. These include car rentals, buses, Amtrak, public transit, hotel shuttles, limo and car service, taxis and their Multi-Modal Transportation Facility (MMTF).

Baltimore International Airport. For information on ground transportation out of BWI check the Ground Transportation page on the airport's website (www.bwi airport.com/en/travel/ground-transportation). The page contains information about taxis, vans and shuttles, rail travel, buses, and car rental phone numbers. Keep in mind, however, that several transportation services do not go beyond the Maryland border into Pennsylvania.

Philadelphia International Airport. For information regarding transportation, please visit the Ground Transportation Information desk located in each baggage claim area. The Ground Transportation Information representative can assist you by providing a list of providers that are authorized to travel to your desti-

Lancaster Airport is ideal for small planes.

nation. To speak with a Ground Transportation Information representative, call 215-937-6958.

REGIONAL AIRPORTS

Lancaster Airport (717-569-1221; www.lancasterairport.com; 500 Airport Road, Lititz, PA 17543). The Lancaster Airport (LNS) is located 6.3 miles (and 18 minutes) north of the city. It is served by Cape Air (866-227-3247) as well as a number of air charter and aircraft rental companies.

Smoketown Airport (717-394-6750; 311 Airport Dr., Smoketown, PA 17576). This small airfield is located about 20 minutes east of Lancaster off PA-340. For those with private planes, this might be a suitable alternative.

New Castle County Airport (302-328-4632; www.newcastleairportilg.com; 151 N. DuPont Highway, New Castle, DE 19720). The New Castle Airport (ILG) is 47 miles (about 1 hour) southeast of Lancaster. Five miles south of Wilmington, it is a general aviation airport close to major transportation arteries (I-95, I-295) and an Amtrak station.

Lehigh Valley Airport (610-266-6000; www.lvia.org; 3311 Airport Road, Allentown, PA 18109). The Lehigh Valley Airport (ABE) is 59 miles (1 hour and 15 minutes) east of Lancaster. This is another "easy-in, easy-out" airport with all the usual amenities. It is served by Allegiant, Delta, Frontier, and United. (At this writing there is an impending merger between American Airlines and USAirways. It is not known how this might affect service at the Lehigh Valley Airport. Please check the airport's website for the most current information.)

BY RENTAL CAR

The major airports all have a wide selection of rental car agencies so you can obtain a set of wheels for your journeys in and around Lancaster County. Be aware that rental car agencies frequently change their rates (several times a day) so it will pay you to shop around to get the best rates (consider comparing rates using www.carrentals.com or www.kayak.com).

Alamo (1-800-354-2322; www.alamo.com)
Avis (1-800-331-1212; www.avis.com)
Budget (1-800-527-0700; www.budget.com)
Dollar (1-800-800-3665; www.dollar.com)
Enterprise (1-800-RENT-A-CAR; www.enterprise.com)
Hertz (1-800-654-3131; www.hertz.com)
National (1-800-227-7368; www.nationalcar.com)
Thrifty (1-800-847-4389; www.thrifty.com)

BY BUS

There are a number of companies that provide bus service to and from Lancaster. Check these out:

Bieber Tourways (1-800-243-2374; www.biebertourways.com; P.O. Box 180, Kutztown, PA 19530). Bieber buses have direct service from Lancaster to and from New York City.

Greyhound Bus Lines (717-397-4861; www.greyhound.com; 53 East McGovern Ave., Lancaster, PA). The old standby has a variety of services in and out of Lancaster.

FAST FACT: Amish girls and boys initiate their search for a spouse shortly after they turn 16.

The Amtrak station in Lancaster awaits your arrival.

Wolf Bus Lines (800-692-7804; www. wolfbus.com; P.O. Box 235, York Springs, PA 17372). Wolf offers bus services to and from New York City directly to Lancaster.

> **F**AST FACT: The Amtrak station in Lancaster handles approximately 560,000 passengers a year.

BY TRAIN

Amtrak (1-800-USA-RAIL; www.amtrak.com) has regular rail service from three Lancaster County locations (Elizabethtown [ELT], Mount Joy [MJY], Lancaster [LNC]) directly to and from both Philadelphia and New York City (with 14 weekday and 8 weekend departures). I frequently take the train from Lancaster (53 East McGovern Ave., Lancaster) into Philadelphia or New York and find the ride to be both comfortable and quick. The Lancaster train station was recently renovated and parking is easy. Rental cars are available and taxis are standing by with each train arrival.

GETTING AROUND LANCASTER COUNTY

Since Lancaster County is primarily rural, there isn't the usual array of big city transportation options for visitors as there might be in a large urban area. However, there are several ways you can get around depending on your time and expense account.

LOCAL BUS SERVICE

Red Rose Transit Authority (717-397-5613; www.redrosetransit.com; 45 Erick Road, Lancaster) offers fixed-route, shared-ride, and special trolley services. It provides public transportation services throughout the city and the county with a fleet of red and white buses. The website has complete information about all routes (both city and county), fares, how to locate bus stops, tourist information, how to ride, safety and security, and bike rack information. All buses have a special "kneeling" feature, which lowers the first step of the bus to curb level. All senior citizens, age 65 and older, ride free.

LOCAL TRANSPORTATION SERVICES

Avis Rent-A-Car (717-569-3185; Lititz).

Conestoga Tours (717-569-1111; www.conestogatours.com).

Lancaster County has lots of unique stores.

Elite Coach (717-733-7710; Ephrata). Elite Coach offers charter service, ground transportation, airport transfers, local shuttles, and long-distance service.

Enterprise Rent-a-Car (717-391-7080; Lancaster).

Executive Coach (717-464-2767; www.executivecoach.net). Executive Coach provides charter service, ground transportation, airport shuttles, pier shuttles, and long-distance service.

Friendly Transportation/Hertz Car Rental (717-393-6666; www.friendly transportation.com). This local company provides ground transportation including private cars, limousines, vans, and motor coaches.

Landis Luxury Coaches (717-859-5466; www.landisenterprises.com). Landis offers a selection of luxury limos and auto rentals.

BY CAR

Travelers through Lancaster County spend a lot of time on I-76, PA-340, US-222, PA-283, or PA-30. Here are some things to know that will ease your automobile travels through the county.

❖ The Pennsylvania Turnpike (I-76) has two exits in Lancaster County: Exit 266 (PA-72—Lebanon/Lancaster) and Exit 286 (US-222 to US-272—Reading/Lancaster). For visitors driving in from other states, this may be the easiest way to get to Lancaster County. Be aware that this route is well traveled and is a significant conduit from and to Pittsburgh and Philadelphia.

❖ PA-30 is the major transportation route into and out of the county. You can use it to get to Lancaster County from Philadelphia and other points east or you can travel PA-30 from York and other points west to get into Lancaster. PA-30 passes just over the northern edge of the city and gets a lot of traffic, including a lot of truck traffic. Because it is a central transportation corridor, it is more than likely that some of your travels will include this major artery.

❖ US-222 is a major north-south highway that enters Lancaster County from the Reading area. It passes over the Pennsylvania Turnpike (I-76) and goes directly into the center of Lancaster city. It comes out the southern end of Lancaster and does a few zigs and zags as it meanders through the southern portions of the county.

❖ PA-283 is the major access route from the Harrisburg area. If you are flying into Harrisburg International Airport (MDT) and rent a car, you will use PA-283 to get into Lancaster County and eventually into Lancaster city (where it links up with US-222 and PA-30).

❖ If you're looking for the commercial Amish attractions, then PA-340 will be your main road. This route strikes out off PA-30 on the eastern part of Lancaster city. It then shoots eastward directly through the quaint towns of Bird-in-Hand and Intercourse and past many of the commercial Amish enterprises and attractions that most likely brought you to Lancaster County in the first place.

A great way to go sightseeing

SIGHTSEEING/TOURS

All-in-One Tours, Cruises & Receptive Services (717-581-5333; www.all-in
-one-tours.com), 1530 Commerce Drive, Suite B, Lancaster.

Brunswick Tours, Inc. (717-361-7541; www.brunswicktours.com), 120 Rid-
geview Road North, Elizabethtown.

Ghost Tours of Lancaster (717-687-6687; www.ghosttour.com), Lancaster and
Strasburg.

Historic Lancaster Walking Tour (717-392-1776; www.historiclancaster
walkingtour.com), 5 West King Street, Lancaster.

ALTERNATE TRANSPORTATION

United States Hot Air Balloon Team (800-763-5987; www.ushotairballoon.com;
Bird-in-Hand). How about a hot-air balloon tour of Lancaster County? You'll get
a bird's-eye view and memories to last a lifetime.

Country Road Scooter and Motorcycle Rentals (717-598-3191; www.country roadscooters.com), 220 North Ronks Road, Bird-in-Hand). Rent a motorcycle or scooter and ride the countryside of Lancaster County and surrounding areas.

Dutch Country Helicopters (717-735-2208; www.flydch.com; Lititz), 500 Airport Road #T, Lititz. Tour the historic Amish country in a Bell 47 helicopter.

Historic Lancaster Walking Tour (717-392-1776; historiclancasterwalkingtour .com; Lancaster). A rewarding, invigorating experience the whole family will enjoy with things you can only see on foot and things you can only see downtown.

Red Rose Segway Tours (717-393-4526; www.redrosesegtours.com; Lancaster). For a real family treat, take a Segway tour of downtown Lancaster. Watch the entire family break into smiles with this unique suggestion!

Strasburg Scooters (717-344-2488; strasburgscooters.com; Ronks). You can explore the Lancaster County countryside on your own scooter.

The Amish have prospered in Lancaster County.

2 Welcome to Amish Country
VISITING THE "PLAIN AND SIMPLE" PEOPLE

The Amish are frequently admired and fascinatingly observed, but rarely understood. Their way of life and beliefs are in opposition to much of what we (the "English") take for granted. However, the fact that they have been able to survive and prosper in modern times is a testament to their beliefs as well as their longevity.

Sixteenth-century Europe was in a state of religious upheaval. In the midst of these changes, a group known as the Brethren formed a new fellowship known as the Anabaptists (or "rebaptizers"). They believed that the church should be a group of voluntary adults, baptized upon confession of faith and separated from the state and world. As a result of their beliefs (especially a church entirely free from state control—a most radical idea), they suffered enormous persecution throughout Europe. Leaders and worshippers were put to death and worship was held in clandestine locations (basements, caves). This persecution led many Anabaptists to develop an attitude of withdrawal from the larger society.

In 1536, a Catholic priest from the Netherlands—Menno Simons—joined the movement. He was a prolific writer and it was through his extensive writings and moderate leadership that widely scattered Anabaptists were brought together. Although there were other leaders who rose during this time, the believers soon became known as "Mennonites."

What we now know as the Amish began back in 1693 with a schism in

> **FAST FACT:** The total U.S. Amish population is approximately 250,000 (as of 2012) living in more than 28 states. The Lancaster County population of Amish is about 31,000 (as of 2013). By 2050, it is predicted that the U.S. Amish population will be in excess of 1 million.

Amish homes frequently have beautiful gardens in front.

Switzerland among a group of Swiss and Alsatian Anabaptists. The divide was led by one Jacob Amman and those who followed him soon became known as Amish. It was their basic belief that the church consist of adults who have voluntarily committed themselves to the fellowship of other like believers. As a result, the purity of the church is maintained.

Both Mennonites and Amish are considered Anabaptists; however, they differ somewhat on their interpretations regarding the purity and faithfulness of the fellowship. As a result, they have split several times over the centuries. Nevertheless, most Amish groups consider themselves to be conservative cousins of the Mennonites.

The Amish are often referred to as "plain and simple" people, and nowhere is this more apparent than in their dress. They wear clothes that are simple in design and color. Men

FAST FACT: The Amish are strict pacifists and are strongly opposed to any form of violence.

and boys wear black suit coats that have no lapels and fasten with hooks and eyes. Their pants are usually held up with suspenders. Shirts are solid colors; they wear brown shoes for work and black shoes for dress up. You'll often see them in straw hats whenever they are outdoors. Young men are clean-shaven; however, as soon as they marry they grow beards, but no mustaches.

> **F**AST FACT: Plain dress is meant to remind one of his or her humble station in life. Plain dress is considered more modest and is meant to keep the believer away from wasteful or sensual garments. This allows the wearer to concentrate on the more productive or worthwhile things of life.

Amish women and girls wear dresses with full skirts of solid colors (no decorations or patterns). Quite often an apron is worn and a cape covers the bodice of the dress. Black shoes are always worn—whether at home or when traveling. Amish women and girls do not cut their hair. They wear it parted in the middle and combed back from the face. They may twist it into a bun at the back of the head or nape of the neck. A head covering, most often white, is always worn indoors and out. No jewelry is ever worn.

Take a buggy ride through Lancaster County.

FAST FACT: Here's a classic Amish proverb: The kind of ancestors you have is not as important as the ones your children have.

The lack of telephones, automobiles, electric appliances, and any modern conveniences by Old Order Amish is both a choice and a requirement of the faith. In addition, the Amish neither purchase any form of insurance nor tap into any form of government assistance such as welfare or Social Security.

As you wend your way through the Amish countryside, you will most likely come upon the ubiquitous buggies of Amish life. Since the Amish reject modern conveniences such as cars and trucks, their preferred method of transportation—the horse and buggy—is most often seen on highways and rural routes, particularly if you travel through Lancaster County on a Sunday. That's when you'll be able to see the buggies lined up in the yard of an Amish farm or forming lines along the road as they return from their weekly worship services. Each buggy will have an orange safety triangle on the back and will be led by a single horse

Amish buggies lined up on Sunday morning

pulling a covered vehicle. The Amish observe all traffic laws, but be aware that their slower pace will require additional attention and consideration from you as you approach them on the road. When nearing and passing a horse-drawn vehicle, remember that horses are unpredictable and even the most road-safe horse can spook at a fast-moving motor vehicle. Be sure to slow down and give buggies and horse-drawn equipment plenty of room when passing. Only pass when legal and safe.

> **F**AST FACT: The Amish are opposed to having their photos taken because they believe that photographs are "graven images." Out of respect for the Amish, please do not take photos of any individuals or groups.

Lancaster County offers a plethora of unique opportunities to learn about the Amish and their way of life. As you tour the area, be respectful of these "plain and simple" people and their beliefs. You will be rewarded with some distinctive insights and memorable adventures available no where else in the country.

BUGGY RIDES

There are a host of companies, large and small, willing to take you on a journey through the Amish countryside in horse-drawn carriages and buggies. These trips may between 30 minutes and one hour with a range of prices (Adults: $15-$22; Children: $10-$15). You'll travel with other folks (about 10 people per buggy) past Amish farms, through covered bridges, and along back-country roads with narration provided by Amish or Mennonite drivers. Most enterprises are open Monday through Saturday (closed on Sundays) from 9 AM-6 PM. Be sure to check for discount coupons in the various newspapers, brochures, and company websites.

A is for Amish Buggy Rides (717-725-8664; www.aisforamishbuggyrides.com), Red Caboose, 312 Paradise Lane, Ronks. This company offers a wide variety of buggy and spring wagon rides. They will also customize a ride specifically for you if there are specific places or events you want to see.

AAA Buggy Rides—Kitchen Kettle Village (717-989-2829; www.AAAbuggyrides.com), 3529 Old Philadelphia Pike, Intercourse. This company has three options for Amish buggy tours: the 35-minute Ultimate Four-Mile Country Buggy Ride, the 55-minute Five-Mile Covered Bridge Tour, and the 60-minute Amish Farm Tour.

> **FAST FACT:** Amish children play with faceless dolls. This supports the Amish's critical perspective on pride and vanity.

Aaron and Jessica's Buggy Rides (717-768-8828; www.amishbuggy rides.com), 3121 Old Philadelphia Pike, Bird-in-Hand. Aaron and Jessica take you right through the middle of Amish country farms, primarily on private roads with no cars. They offer family discounts, group rides, and special offers.

Abe's Buggy Rides (717-392-1794; www.abesbuggyrides.com), 2596 Old Philadelphia Pike, Bird-in-Hand. Abe's has five tours that pass a number of Amish farms, an Amish one-room school house, and other sites dating back to the 1700s.

Amish Barn Buggy Rides (717-768-8828; www.amishbarnbuggyrides.com), 3029 Old Philadelphia Pike, Bird-in-Hand. During this 20- to 25-minute ride, you'll pass a blacksmith's shop, the Buggy Factory, an Amish school, a furniture maker, orchards, and various farms.

Ed's Buggy Rides (717-687-0360; www.edsbuggyrides.com), 253 Hartman Bridge Road (Route 896), Ronks. This 3-mile tour through the Pennsylvania Dutch country landscape offers glimpses of the Amish along hilly back roads in an authentic Amish buggy. This is the only buggy ride that does not travel on main roads.

Travel back roads as the Amish do.

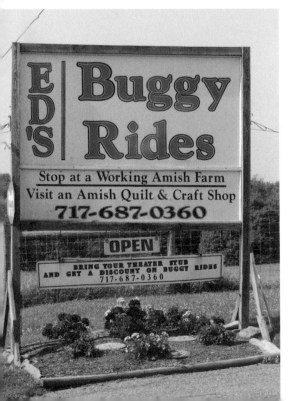

HOMES AND FARMS

You and your family can get a guided tour through an authentic Amish house by a knowledgeable guide. You'll learn about the Amish way of life, their daily activities and chores, and some of the tools and equipment they use both in the house and on the property. Many of these sites have outbuildings and farm exhibits that offer additional insights into the Amish way of life. Most are open seven days a week with staggered

The Amish Farm and House

hours (usually 9 AM–6 PM) depending on the season. Admission rates range from about $6 for children to $9 for adults.

> **FAST FACT:** There are approximately 4,800 Amish farms in Lancaster County.

The Amish Country Homestead at Plain & Fancy Farm (717-768-3600, ext. 210; www.AmishExperience.com), 3121 Old Philadelphia Pike (Route 340), Bird-in-Hand. Inside, you'll learn about Amish traditions and practices, plain clothing, and life without electricity. Touring the Homestead provides you with an opportunity to observe how the fictional Fisher family lives from day to day.

Amish Farm and House (717-394-6185; www.amishfarmandhouse.com), 2395 Lincoln Highway East (Route 30), Lancaster. This site offers a tour of a 1805 farmhouse, a 15-acre farm with out-buildings, farm animals, walking trails, farm

The Amish Village

exhibits, a covered bridge, a blacksmith's shop, and a one-room schoolhouse. It has been in operation since 1955.

The Amish Village (717-687-8511; www.TheAmishVillage.net), 199 Hartman Bridge Road, Ronks. The Amish Village will provide you with an authentic look at today's Amish lifestyle. Located on 12 acres, it lets visitors tour an authentic Amish property, including a one-room schoolhouse, blacksmith shop, smokehouse market, and several outbuildings.

COMMERCIAL AMISH TOURS

These tours provide journeys through the Amish countryside—all in the comfort of an air-conditioned bus or mini-bus. You'll get a most knowledgeable guide (not Amish, since they are not permitted to drive motor vehicles), who will lead a 90-minute narrated tour—an up-close and personal glimpse into Amish life. You'll get a flavor of the real Lancaster County as you learn the area's history, culture, and local stories and see a variety of Amish farms, schools, and houses. Prices range from about $20 to $50 (depending on length of time) for adults and $15 to $20 for kids. Most operate seven days a week.

Amish Country Tours (717-768-3600; www.AmishExperience.com), Plain & Fancy Farm, 3121 Old Philadelphia Pike (Route 340), Bird-in-Hand. This 90-minute farmlands tour includes a stop at an Amish property, and (frequently) a bake shop, roadside stand, or quilt shop on a farm, so that visitors can interact with the Amish. This tour is part of a complete overview of Amish culture for visitors. Farmland tours are on a 14-passenger "mini-shuttle."

Amish Farm and House Countryside Tours (717-394-6185; www.amishfarm andhouse.com), 2395 Lincoln Highway East, Lancaster. This company has been in operation since 1955 and offers one of the most comprehensive bus tours of Amish country. The guides are all knowledgeable and offer insights about Amish schoolhouses, buggies, barns, farms, historic homes, and the beautiful farmlands.

Take a bus ride along the back roads of Amish country.

Amish Village Backroads Bus Tour
(717-687-8511; www.TheAmish
Village.com), 199 Hartman Bridge
Road, Ronks (Strasburg). This 1.5-
hour tour will take you off the beaten
path, past working farms and along
picturesque country roads. You'll get

> **F**AST FACT: Many Amish
> favor chiropractic care or
> herbal medicines. They will
> only go to a medical doctor
> when absolutely necessary.

a behind-the-scenes look at Amish life—their history, customs, beliefs, and traditions. Each bus tour includes at least at one stop at unique locations such as an
Amish home, quilt shop, pretzel bakery, or bake shop.

Bob Neff Tours (717-397-0000; www.bobnefftours.com), 1525 Oregon Pike,
Suite 2201. Whether you are looking for history, music, art, Amish farms, quilts,
small towns, or scenery, this company will design customized itineraries as well
as make reservations for lodging, meals, attractions, and transportation.

JB Amish Tours (717-725-2357; www.jbamishtours.com), Lancaster County.
This company offers custom-designed one-on-one tours, as well as planned
tours for very large groups. All of the guides grew up in Lancaster County and
know Amish people personally.

Mennonite Information Center (717-299-0954; www.mennoniteinfoctr.com),
2209 Millstream Road, Lancaster. Arrange a tour with your own personal
guide—a native of Lancaster County who will travel with you in your own car.
Your guide will take you to about three places that interest you including farms,
quilt shops, bakeries, or root beer stands. Rates start at $49 for a two-hour tour
in a private car and go up to $120 for a three-hour coach tour for large groups.

Off the Beaten Track Amish Country Quilt Tours (717-575-1349), Greenfield
Drive, Leola. If you're into quilts, then this is your tour. A knowledgeable, experienced guide will ride with you in your car and lead you to several quaint Amish
quilt shops throughout the Lancaster County countryside.

Old Order Amish Tours (717-299-6535; www.oldorderamishtours.com), 63
Eastbrook Road (Route 896 North), Ronks. These tours are authentic, private,
and absolutely respectful to the Amish. One of the knowledgeable guides will
show you sites and present the Amish culture in a unique and unforgettable way.
You'll visit a working Old Order Amish farm, where you'll see and learn how
the plain people still plow their fields with Belgian workhorses and live without
electricity.

A typical Amish house

SELF-GUIDED TOURS

One of the best ways to see the farms and houses of the Amish is to head out on your own along back-country roads and seldom traveled byways. Exploring on your own will give you some unique opportunities to see the "plain and simple" life away from all the glitz that sometimes takes over the commercial enterprises along Routes 340 and 30. Don't worry about getting lost—eventually most of the rural roads will return you back into Lancaster. Besides, some of the best discoveries I've made in Lancaster County have been when my wife and I had no idea where we were going and wound up at an antiques barn or roadside stand that was in nobody's travel guide or brochure.

On all three of the following tours you will see a number of Amish homes and farms. Here are some things to look for that will help you differentiate Amish homes/farms from those of the "English" (everyone else who is not Amish). In an Amish home/farm:

✣ There are absolutely no electric wires or telephone lines going into the house.

✣ There will usually be dark green shades or simple white curtains on the windows.

✣ There will be a dirt road or gravel driveway (no asphalt).

✣ There will be a clothesline (clothes are dried outside).

✣ The property will be well kept and well maintained.

✣ There will often be a covered porch on the front of the house.

✣ Homes and out-buildings will be simply painted—most are white, however, they may be in tones of brown or gray; bright colors are not used.

✣ There is often an expansive flower and/or vegetable garden in the front yard.

✣ There may be a windmill and/or several shade trees on the property.

AMISH FARM TOUR #1

Estimated length: 16 miles
Estimated time: 1–1.5 hours

Begin this tour in the town of Bird-in-Hand. Head east on PA-340 for approximately 0.8 mile and make a right turn on South Weavertown Road (there will be a gray "English" house on the corner). Just after the turn, there will be a white Amish home on the right. Slow down and notice the features outlined in the box above.

Continue down South Weavertown Road and after 0.4 mile make a right at the T in the road. The road curves around to the left and you will come to another T in the road. Make a right turn at this T (onto Irishtown Road). Just before you turn onto Irishtown Road, you will notice an Amish farm on the left and just after that turn will be another Amish farm on the right (just before you make a curve to the left).

You may be surprised to see that many Amish farms grow immense fields of tobacco—a very profitable crop. The Amish are very conscientious farmers and regularly rotate their crops of corns, alfalfa, and tobacco.

Tobacco is grown on many Amish farms.

At the next stop sign, make a left turn onto North Ronks Road. You will then drive under an overpass and find yourself in the tiny town of Ronks. Just on the other side of Ronks you will pass another Amish farm on the left (white house, red barn).

You'll come to the intersection of North Ronks Road and US-30 (Lincoln Highway East). Travel through the intersection and continue on Ronks Road. The first farm you see on the right is an Amish farm (red and white house). Again, you'll notice that there is no electricity—no telephone wires or electric wires going into the house.

Continue on Ronks Road for 1.1 miles and turn right (you will have passed Herr Road on the right) off

> **FAST FACT:** Each Amish community may have a dress code that the community must follow. These codes may vary from one community to the next.

An Amish schoolhouse on PA-741

Ronks Road at the stop sign. After 0.2 mile there will be a Y in the road. Take the right-hand part of the Y (Paradise Road). You'll notice a brick home on the left (there may be a horse and buggy in the garage) and a tobacco field on the right. As you continue down the road, you'll see the Red Caboose Motel on the left (definitely not Amish).

You'll come up to an intersection (with a traffic signal) with PA-741 (Gap Road). Turn left onto PA-741. You'll soon see several Amish farms on the right side of the road. Notice the multiple buildings—many of which are painted white. You'll also notice a sprinkling of "English" homes here and there along the road.

After 2.5 miles you'll pass by an Amish schoolhouse on the left—a white building with a picket fence all around. One of the most iconic symbols of Amish life, the one-room schoolhouse, can be found throughout the Lancaster County countryside. Formal education for the Amish goes up to grade eight and classes are taught by young girls (typically 17 to 20 years old) who were good students while they were in school. After grade eight, the young are expected to work in the fields (boys) or tend to various household chores (girls).

At this point the road has a new name—Strasburg Road. Look around and, depending on the time of year you are traveling, you'll see lots of greenery— gently rolling hills and farmland as far as the eye can see. Most of the land will be farmed with vehicles with steel wheels and drawn by horses or mules—no mechanization whatsoever. Houses, too, are all plain and simple—nothing fancy, no decorations. The fences may be white or unpainted, and the landscaping is simple. The emphasis is more on practicality than it is on decoration.

About 1.2 miles from the school house will be **Fisher's Produce**—an expansive roadside stand on the left side of the road. This is where you want to stop and get some great Amish food. It offers an incredible variety of canned goods— everything from honey to green tomato relish to elderberry jelly to vegetable

Fisher's Produce has lots of Lancaster County goodies.

F AST FACT: The average Amish family has seven children. About 25 percent of all households have ten or more children.

soup to garlic chips to chow-chow to apple butter. You'll also get a great selection of produce (depending on the season). Whatever you do, be sure to get some homemade root beer and an ever-classic whoopie pie.

Turn your vehicle around and head back on PA-741 (Strasburg Road); 2.5 miles from Fisher's Produce you'll make a right turn onto Black Horse Road. After 0.6 mile on Black Horse Road, you'll come to another Amish schoolhouse on the left. This one, too, is a one-room tan-colored schoolhouse with a simple fence all around.

You'll soon arrive at the intersection of Black Horse Road and US-30 (Lincoln Highway East). You are now in Paradise, a classic Lancaster County small town (population: 1,028), with an abundance of brick homes, along with a profusion of traffic zipping along the main route. This is a town with charm to spare, so you may want to stop and roam through some of the shops for an authentic Pennsylvania Dutch gift.

The Myer Homestead, established in 1759

Make a left turn onto US-30 and then after 0.2 mile make a quick right turn on Leacock Road (there's a Wells Fargo bank on the corner). After half a mile, you'll see an Amish bookstore (Gordonville Book Store) on the right side of the road.

Continue another mile and you'll find another one-room school house on the left. This one has a white fence around it and a small ball field in the rear. Drive for another 0.4 mile and you'll come upon the Leacock Shoe Store on the left. This store is frequented by the Amish, who shop here for shoes and clothing.

Drive for another 0.4 mile (from the shoe store) and you'll eventually come to the intersection of Old Leacock Road and PA-340. Make a left turn onto PA-340 and drive for 1.6 miles back to the town of Bird-in-Hand.

AMISH FARM TOUR #2

Estimated length: 9 miles
Estimated time: 1 hour

This tour begins in the village of Intercourse. After you have toured this fascinating town (see Chapter 4), turn your car onto PA-772 N (also known as West Newport Road). After 0.7 mile, you'll see an Amish farm on the left. This is one of the larger farms in the area and you'll note several out-buildings and a sophisticated farming operation in place. Travel 0.4 mile more, and another large Amish farm will be on the left. Look for a large assembly of horses, mules, and other field animals.

Continue your drive on PA-772 (W. Newport Road). PA-772 will eventually bend around to the left, but you'll want to continue your drive straight ahead on Hess Road (be careful—the sign may be difficult to see). Notice the farmlands all around as you travel north on Hess Road. You'll see a profusion of Amish farms on both sides of the road. When you come to a stop sign, make a left turn onto Eby Road (there will be an Amish farm directly ahead.).

After 0.2 mile, you'll pass by Hess Road on the right—be sure to stay on East Eby Road. In a very short distance, you'll see an Amish schoolhouse on the left (a tan building with a chain-link fence). After another 0.2 mile you'll come to the Myer Homestead with its graveyard on the right. This would be a good opportunity to park your car off the road and walk over to the iron fence surrounding this homestead,

FAST FACT: In most Amish households, the day begins around 4:30 am. Usually everyone turns in for the night around 8:30 pm.

which was originally established in 1759. Just outside the perimeter of the fence (and close to the road) is the following historical marker:

> Herein lies Abraham C. Myer (deceased 1792) and his heirs. Of German descent, he arrived 1758 and purchased 100 acres of land to the north and east of this point. Eight generations of farmers followed and were a stable influence as community and church leaders, pump and furniture makers, blacksmiths, inventors and educators. Abram Hess married Caroline Myer in 1894 and continued farming followed by their son Titus M. Hess (deceased 1991) and wife, Anna Haldeman, their six children and grandchildren.
>
> *In 1976 the farm was identified by the U.S. Department of the Interior as a Bicentennial Family farm. After 237 years of farming in 1994 the heirs donated an easement to the Lancaster Farmland Trust as a farmland forever.*

Immediately after the graveyard (on the right) is **Riehl's Quilts and Crafts**. This is where you want to be if you're in the market for an authentic Amish quilt. The selection here is unparalleled and the quality exceptional. After leaving Riehl's make a right turn back onto East Eby Road and then a quick left onto Stumptown Road. As you journey along this road, notice the expanse of Amish farms off to your left and all the way to the horizon. If the daylight is right, you'll see an incredible sight of Pennsylvania agriculture as it once was . . . and is currently maintained by the Amish. This is a calendar view—one that just can't be duplicated anywhere else. Stop and enjoy the vista; it is truly memorable.

You'll shortly arrive at the intersection of Stumptown Road and PA-772 (Newport Road). Across the road, on the southeast corner of this intersection is a unique Lancaster County landmark offering visitors a magical glimpse into the past. The **Mascot Roller Mills**, originally built in the mid-1730s, was an economic and social center where Amish and Mennonite farmers had their corn ground into cornmeal, exchanged wheat for flour, bought and sold wheat at the end of the season, and had their grain ground into animal feed. What you will see here is a documentation of the rural milling industry in the United States—from its earliest beginnings as a business enterprise to

FAST FACT: Here's another Amish proverb: To grow old gracefully, you must start when you are young.

its current place as a living museum. While most mills throughout the U.S. have fallen into disuse and disrepair, this structure has been lovingly preserved by the Ressler Mill Foundation in order to educate the public about grain milling and a way of life quite distant from our own.

Also located at the site is the **Ressler Family Home**—the house where the owners of the mill lived for more than two centuries. Visit the home and you will step back into the pages of history. The house, home to three generations of the Ressler family, and its contents have been faithfully preserved (there are no replicas and re-creations here) as a window into 19th- and 20th century rural living. Here you'll see a coal-fired stove, Mother Ressler's rocking chair, a bride's box, and period antiques that were part of the home's furnishings in a bygone era. Step through the home and you will quickly get a sense of what the "good old days" were really like.

After departing the Ressler Family Home and Mascot Roller Mills, turn right onto PA-772 and return to the town of Intercourse.

AMISH FARM TOUR #3

Estimated length: 21 miles
Estimated time: 1.5 hours

This tour starts on the east end of Lancaster at the intersection of US-30 and PA-896. To begin, head south from the traffic signal on PA-896 S (toward Strasburg). After 1 mile, make a left turn onto Bachmantown Road. You will begin to notice several Amish farms—particularly on the right side of the road. Take note of the plain exterior of the buildings and the fact that most all are painted white. Half a mile down Bachmantown Road, there will be a small house on the right side. This is known as a "dotty house"—a home especially for grandparents or for retired individuals (most Amish retire at about age 50—although their perception of retirement is quite different from that of the "English"). There will be another dotty house right next to the first one. You'll also notice long fields on both sides of the road.

Three-tenths of a mile after the dotty homes, slow down and look carefully on the left side of the road and you may see an Amish phone booth (wooden, white, and about six-feet tall) set back from the road about 10 yards and along the right side of a dirt driveway that leads to an Amish farm. The Amish do not have phones in their homes (phones are viewed as an intrusion into the privacy and sanctity of the family), but they are allowed to make and receive calls in

Herr's Mill Bridge has seen better days.

other locations. Amish phones must be in a "booth" or small out-building placed far enough from the house as to make its use inconvenient. These phones are often used by more than one family.

After the phone booth, there will be several other Amish farms and homes on both the left and right. Take notice of all the fruit trees in this area. About 0.4 mile after the phone booth, you'll come to a stop sign. Make a right turn onto Ronks Road. You'll see a number of Amish homes mixed in with "English" homes. There will be a farm on the right side (red barn, grayish house) and an Amish home on the left. After 0.4 mile you will pass **Herr's Mill Covered Bridge** (also known as the Soudersburg Bridge). This bridge was built in 1844 and is one of the few double-span, double-arch bridges remaining in the United States. It also has an unusual side entrance that was originally used to measure the level of the stream in relation to the bridge. Due to its present condition, however, you will not be able to drive across it.

About 0.8 mile from the bridge, you will come to a Y in the road. Bear left at the stop sign. Soon after, there will be a farm on the left with a large white house. Six-tenths of a mile after the Y you will discover a one-room schoolhouse on the left side of the road. This school has a tall chain-link fence surrounding it.

> **F**AST FACT: There are more than 200 one-room schoolhouses in Lancaster County.

You'll notice several Amish homes on this portion of the road, including a fruit farm on the right side. About 0.8 mile after the schoolhouse you will come to a stop sign (Cherry Hill Road). After stopping, proceed through the intersection to Singer Avenue and bear left. You'll soon arrive at another stop sign (US-30). Make a right turn on US-30 and you will be traveling through the small town of Paradise (make sure you send your friends back home a postcard indicating that you spent part of your vacation in Paradise). In 0.2 mile make a left turn onto Leacock Road (there will be a Wells Fargo bank on the left corner of the intersection).

A popular Lancaster County resident

After half a mile, you'll travel past the Gordonville Book Store; continue 0.9 mile and you will discover a white schoolhouse on the left side of the road. It will have a white wooden fence all around it. Just past the schoolhouse, make a right onto Harvest Road. Feast your eyes on all the farms and fields of corn along this road. After about a mile, make a right turn onto Belmont Road. You will see several Amish farms on both sides of the road.

Then, 1.2 miles after you turn onto Belmont Road, you'll come to an Amish produce stand on the right. If it is open, you definitely want to stop and peruse the canned goods, vegetable soups, jams, pies, cookies, bakery items, whoopee pies, lemonade, homemade root beer, and birdhouses. It is truly a feast for the eyes and the stomach. Soon after the produce stand, you will travel through **Eshleman's Mill Covered Bridge** (also known as Paradise Bridge and/or Leaman Place Bridge). This bridge, over the Pequea Creek, was originally built in 1845 and rebuilt in 1893. It is 113-feet long and has been reinforced with concrete in recent years.

About 0.4 mile after the bridge, you will see an Amish shoe store on the left side of the road. Just after the shoe store you will arrive at a traffic signal (US-30). Continue straight ahead on Belmont Road; 0.7 mile after the traffic signal look

The kids will love staying at the Red Caboose Motel.

to the left and you will notice a small mountain of gray rock off to the horizon. This is an enormous pile of limestone. An abundant supply of limestone is one of the reasons why this area is so rich agriculturally. Limestone is a sedimentary rock composed of skeletal fragments of ancient marine organisms. Pulverized limestone is used agriculturally as a soil conditioner to neutralize acidic soils.

Eight-tenths of a mile farther down Belmont Road, you will come to a school-house on the right (it will be on the corner of Belmont Road and PA-741). Continue straight ahead on Belmont Road. Notice the picturesque scenery all around and if you are lucky, you'll see the farmers working in their fields. Depending on the time of day or season of the year you are traveling, you may come upon Amish families traveling in their horse-drawn buggies, carriages, or wagons. About 1.8 miles from the Belmont Road/PA-714 intersection you will arrive at a stop sign (PA-896 N/Georgetown Road). Make a right turn onto PA-896 N.

Exactly 1.9 miles later, take a look to your right. You're likely to see one of the most stunning vistas in all of Lancaster County. As far as the eye can see, you'll discover a spread of farms, farmhouses, and fields in every direction. If you can find a place to pull off the road, this would be the time to get out your camera and begin snapping away. This is what Amish country is all about.

After 0.6 mile, make a right onto Paradise Lane. You'll now be driving through some of those beautiful farms you saw up on the ridge. In about 1 mile, you'll cross over Gap Road and shortly after you will notice the Red Caboose Motel and the National Toy Train Museum (neither of which are Amish) on the right side of the road. About 0.7 mile after the train museum, you will come to a Y in the road. Make a hard left turn (this is Fairview Road, but there is no street sign). Then make an almost-immediate right turn onto North Star Road. You'll notice some dairy farms, tobacco barns, a quilt shop, and a schoolhouse (a former "English" school, now an Amish school). Three-tenths of a mile after the school-house you'll arrive at a stop sign (PA-896).

Make a right turn onto PA-896 and 2.2 miles later you will arrive back at your starting point (the intersection of US-30 and PA-896). You're sure to remember this trip as one that combines both past and present into an unforgettable journey through Amish country.

Downtown Lancaster welcomes you.

3 Lancaster City
LOTS TO DO, LOTS TO SEE

efore getting into the history and background of Lancaster, it's important to know the right way to pronounce "Lancaster." You'll appear less like a tourist and more like a native if you say the name of the city and the county correctly. The locals pronounce "Lancaster" as *LANK*-*iss*-*ter* (a more British pronunciation), rather than the typical American pronunciation: *LAN*-*kast*-*er*. (Those of you from the West Coast are no doubt familiar with the "Lancaster" in California that uses the American pronunciation.)

Now that we have our diction lesson out of the way, it's interesting to note that the original name for the city was "Hickory Town"—not very romantic; but much easier to say. However, sometime after its founding in 1734, it was renamed after the English town of Lancaster in England. Its symbol, the red rose (Lancaster is often referred to as the Red Rose City), is from the House of Lancaster. Lancaster was initially incorporated as a borough in 1742 and as a city in 1818.

During the Revolutionary War, Lancaster was an important munitions center. Afterward, the city rose to become an iron-foundry center. In the 1800s Lancaster began to diversify and embraced a number of businesses and industries such as textiles, manufacturing, furniture, silverware, clocks, and grist mills. As the city moved into the 20th century, other

FAST FACT: Lancaster City was the nation's capital for one day, September 27, 1777, when the Continental Congress held a session at the Court-house (the British had captured Philadelphia and the Continental Congress fled to the safety of Lancaster). The city also served as the capital of Pennsylvania from 1799 to 1812.

industries were established including cigar-making, metal-working, automobile parts and, eventually, a vibrant tourist trade.

As you begin your journey down the streets and through the history of this energetic town, you will be able to glimpse and appreciate all that Lancaster once was and all that it is now. This is a city that tastefully celebrates its history and embraces its present. To say that it has something for everyone would be an understatement; to say that it offers visitors a wealth of discoveries and diversity of experiences would truly make it an original "All-America City"—a designation it achieved in 2000.

Let's begin our exploration of Lancaster with a historical stroll through the bustling and dynamic downtown area.

WALKING TOUR OF DOWNTOWN LANCASTER

Estimated length: 1–1.5 miles
Estimated time: 2 hours

The walk described below offers you an up close and personal look at some of the most significant features of Lancaster City. The diversity of people, the diversity of architecture, and the diversity of history will all be evident in this journey.

First, you'll need a place to park. Here's a suggestion: the super-sized Prince Street Garage at the corner of Prince Street and Orange Street in downtown Lancaster. You'll always find a space here and it's centrally located. After parking your car, walk east on West Orange Street and turn right onto Market Street. After half a block, you'll be right in front of **Lancaster Central Market**. Walk through the market and you'll feel like you've been transported to a European

Lancaster Central Market

bazaar. Stands and booths overflow with an eclectic array of foods that will tantalize any palate and please any chef. Here you can discover meats, poultry, seafood, fruits, vegetables, candy, flowers, dairy products, bulk foods, baskets, household items, bread, salads, homemade horseradish, Middle Eastern food, Greek food, German food, fresh ground coffee, bakery items, and organic products galore. Central Market has been here since 1730 and for over 275 years it has been the place to meet and the place to buy.

After you've visited Central Market and filled your grocery bags with all those sumptuous delights, it's time to begin our walking tour. Depart the Market on King Street and head east toward Penn Square. Make a right turn on South Queen Street and walk down to 24-26 S. Queen Street. Here you'll see the **Yeates House** (now the Literacy Council of Lancaster-Lebanon Counties). This particular home was constructed in about 1765. Its owner, Jasper Yeates, was a

The Yeates House

delegate to the U.S. Constitutional Convention in 1787 and also served as a U.S. Supreme Court justice.

Cross the street and walk back up South Queen Street to Penn Square and enter the **Marriott Hotel**. Proceed down the stairway or escalator and into the

Lancaster County Convention Center. Near the back you'll come up to a bowed exterior wall directly across from Freedom Hall. This wall was once the rear wall of the **William Montgomery Mansion** constructed in 1804. Montgomery was a well-known lawyer in the early 1800s. Continue down the stairs and you'll come across buildings that are now part of the Convention Center. These buildings were once owned by Thaddeus Stevens—a prominent abolitionist, lawyer, and congressman who had a major influence on the passage of the 13th and 14th Amendments to the U.S. Constitution. The one building on the corner was the **Kleiss Saloon**—a popular hangout in its day. Immediately next to it was **Stevens's house and law office**. Look carefully past the barricades and/or windows and you will note two cisterns (along with several artifacts). There is considerable evidence to prove that these cisterns were used to hide runaway slaves along the Underground Railroad. When I visited, these sites were still being developed as part of an Underground Railroad museum.

Also part of this site is the **Lydia Hamilton Smith House**. Smith was a housekeeper who worked for Thaddeus Stevens. She kept his house and managed his business affairs. It is also suspected that she too was a "conductor" for the Underground Railroad—assisting Stevens in helping slaves seeking safe passage northward.

Walk back through the convention center and the lobby of the Marriott. Exit the building, make a left turn, and stroll back down South Queen Street. Make a left turn on West Vine Street and head east on Vine. When you get to South Duke Street make a right turn and begin to wander. You are now in a part of Lancaster known as Old Town. Here you will discover an amazing variety of homes dating from the mid-1700s to the early 1900s. Many of these classic homes are part of the "City of Lancaster Historic District" and are scattered among tree-lined streets and brick sidewalks. As you stroll through this section of town, you'll see a variety of architectural styles representing almost two centuries of urban living. Interestingly, these private residences were scheduled for demolition in the 1970s but were saved from the wrecker's ball through the efforts of many citizens.

After leaving Old Town, walk north on South Duke Street. In half a block you'll come up to the **Evangelical Lutheran Church of the Holy Trinity** on your right. The congregation for this church was originally organized in 1730, although the church wasn't constructed until 1767. This particular church is the only one in the city that has survived from colonial times.

You can enter the church through the doors on Mifflin Street. When you do, note the façade of the organ on the balcony. This was the case of the original organ installed in 1774. Also note the stained-glass window *(The Crucifixion)*, which was created in 1913 by none other than Louis Comfort Tiffany.

As you come up to the corner of King and Duke streets, look to your left and you will see the **County Courthouse** on the northwest corner of these two streets. Originally built in 1852-1854, it is certainly an imposing edifice among the buildings in this section of town.

Make a right turn onto East King Street. Immediately look for two residences (110 and 112 East King Street). Note that these two homes were originally constructed in the early 1760s. Continue a short distance down King Street and you'll come to one of the classic businesses in Lancaster—the **Demuth Tobacco Shop** (114 East King Street). This particular enterprise has been selling tobacco products since long before the Surgeon General posted any warnings on packages of some of those items. In fact, this shop has been in operation since 1770 (it may have provided cigars for some of our early patriots) and is the oldest operating tobacconist in America—a testament to the country's persistent love affair with tar and nicotine.

Make a U-turn on King Street and return to Duke Street. Make a right turn and head north on Duke. On the right side of Duke (across from the courthouse) you'll notice an array of law offices, sometimes referred to as Lawyers Row. Observe carefully and you'll note that many of these law offices are former colonial dwellings that have been put to quite another use. Pay particular attention to the **Muhlenberg House** (33 N. Duke Street) which is also a law office. This building was a parsonage for Reverend Gotthilf Heinrich Ernst Muhlenberg, who was the pastor for Trinity Lutheran Church from 1780 to 1815.

Continue your walk up Duke Street. On the northeast corner of Duke and Orange streets, you'll see **St. James Episcopal Church**—a building erected in the 1820s. The church was founded in 1744 as the Anglican Church (Church of England). Before the onset of the American Revolution, the rector of the church was Thomas Barton. Reverend Barton was a loyal subject of the King of England as well as of the church. Although there were many American patriots in his congregation, he could not openly condone their actions. So he closed up the church and conducted church services in a secret location. Take a walk through the church cemetery and you will see the grave markers of a number of notable Lancasterians. These include Edward Hand, surgeon to George Washington;

The Muhlenberg House

Edward Shippen, father-in-law of Benedict Arnold; Robert Coleman, a delegate to the 1787 Constitutional Convention; and his daughter, Ann Coleman, the one-time fiancée of President James Buchanan.

Make a right turn on Orange Street and head eastward. As you will discover, Orange Street offers a most incredible visual treat.

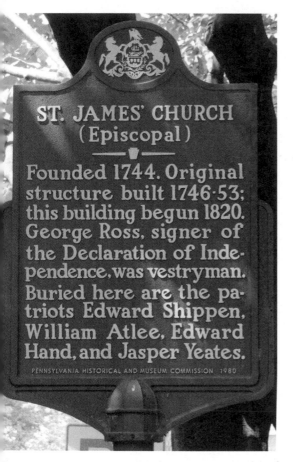

St. James Church is more than 250 years old.

On the northwest corner of Orange and Lime Streets is the **Shippen House** (now the YMCA). Edward Shippen was a lawyer and a judge and lived in this house from 1751 to 1781. Shippen was the grandfather of Peggy Shippen Arnold, the wife of Benedict Arnold.

Continue your walk to the **home of Dr. Thomas Bond** (207 East Orange Street). This home was constructed around 1780. Dr. Bond and Benjamin Franklin were instrumental in establishing the Pennsylvania Hospital.

The **Christopher Marshall Home** (215 East Orange Street) housed Marshall and his family from 1777 to 1797. Marshall moved here from Philadelphia specifically to avoid being captured by British armies roaming the City of Brotherly Love.

The **Timothy Matlock Home** (222 East Orange Street) housed the Matlock family from 1799 to 1812. Matlock was the clerk to the Continental Congress in 1776. It was he who penned the original copy of the *Declaration of Independence* that was signed by the members of Congress. That original is now in the National Archives. He also penned several other federal documents and decrees, including George Washington's 1775 commission as Commander-in-Chief.

The **Baker-Stauffer House** (235 East Orange) was built around 1830 for noted coach maker John Baker. After it was purchased by David McNeely Stauffer in 1882, it was substantially enlarged.

The **Passmore House** (247 East Orange) was constructed sometime prior to 1760. It was the home of Lancaster's first mayor. Look closely and you'll notice an oversized front door. That's because "his honor" was an oversized individual—more than 400 pounds oversize.

The **Andrew Jackson Steinman Mansion** (301 East Orange) sits at the corner of Orange and Shippen streets. It was constructed in 1882 for newspaper magnate Andrew Jackson Steinman. One can only imagine that Mr. Steinman's ego was as large as his house.

After viewing the Steinman Mansion, make a U-turn and return along Orange Street. Continue walking past Duke Street and then past Queen Street until you come to North Prince Street. Turn right on North Prince and walk past the entrance for the Prince Street Garage. Shortly after, you will see the **Sehner-Ellicott-von Hess House** (123 North Prince Street). This building (now the Historic Preservation Trust) was originally built about 1767. In 1800 it was the home of Andrew Ellicott, who was an engineer and surveyor. Ellicott was commissioned by President Thomas Jefferson to train Meriwether Lewis before he and William Clark set out on their exploration of the recently obtained Louisiana Purchase. This building also has a small museum open to the public.

After viewing the Sehner-Ellicott-von Hess House, return to the Prince Street Garage to retrieve your car.

The Andrew Jackson Steinman Mansion

HISTORIC SITES AND ORGANIZATIONS

Lancaster is a city built on history. If you're looking to steep yourself in some of the historical traditions of this city, then you can't go wrong with any of the following organizations and their impressive displays. As you tour the city, take the time to stop at any one of these places and you will come away with a deeper appreciation of the roots of this vibrant community.

Lancaster County's Historical Society (717-392-4633; www.lancasterhistory. org), 4 West King Street, Lancaster. A variety of events and education programs, a detailed exhibit center, and loads of information (photographs, newspapers, oral histories, personal diaries) about the historical roots of Lancaster County can be found here.

Lancaster Mennonite Historical Society (717-393-9745; www.lmhs.org), 2215 Millstream Road, Lancaster. Lancaster Mennonite Historical Society "preserves and interprets the culture and context of Anabaptist-related faith communities connected to Lancaster County." They are also a great resource for information and tours of the surrounding area.

President James Buchanan's Wheatland (717-392-8721; www.lancasterhistory .org), 1120 Marietta Avenue, Lancaster. The home of our country's 15th president is spectacular and gracious. Buchanan was the only president from Pennsylvania. His house was designated a national Historic Landmark in 1961 and listed on the National Register of Historic Places in 1966. Its setting in a copse of trees is picture-postcard perfect—especially in the fall.

> **FAST FACT:** James Buchanan was America's only bachelor president.

Rock Ford Plantation (717-392-7223; www.rockfordplantation.org), 881 Rock Ford Road, Lancaster. Standing on the wooded banks of the Conestoga River, this Georgian-style brick mansion is a remarkably preserved remnant of 18th-century living. It was the colonial estate of Edward Hand, who rose to become Adjutant General to George Washington in 1781.

MUSEUMS

There are thousands of treasures to be found in the museums of Lancaster. Combine a few of these city museums with some of the county museums listed later in this book (see Chapter 9) and you'll have some unparalleled experiences.

The Demuth Museum celebrates the noted artist Charles Demuth.

Demuth Museum (717-299-9940; www.demuth.org), 120 East King Street, Lancaster. This museum is dedicated to an appreciation of the art work and legacy of American modernist Charles Demuth. The museum has an innovative program of exhibitions, education, scholarship, and collections.

North Museum is a terrific family adventure

Lancaster Museum of Art (717 394-3497; www.lmapa.org), 135 North Lime Street, Lancaster. The museum is located in a Greek Revival-style mansion built in 1845-46. The museum's programs focus on exhibitions of contemporary art by regional and national artists.

North Museum of Natural History and Science (717-291-3941; www.northmuseum.org), 400 College Avenue, Lancaster. This is a premier museum with an amazing variety of offerings. Collections include birds, rocks and minerals, Native American artifacts, and a planetarium. There are many education programs and summer camps along with a host of temporary and permanent exhibits.

Pennsylvania Guild Craftsmen (717-431-8706; www.pacrafts.org) 335 North Queen St Lancaster. Here you can take classes, workshops, and seminars. Learn a new skill or craft. Shop their store, see their exhibits, and get information on all the craft fairs scheduled throughout Lancaster County during the year.

ART GALLERIES & STUDIOS

Just one visit to downtown Lancaster and the plethora of galleries scattered throughout the city and you'll have an arts experience like no other. No matter the genre, style or medium, you're sure to find distinctive paintings, classic pottery, dynamic weavings, and exuberant art of every kind. Follow one of the popular gallery walks (below) and you'll have an experience you'll be talking about for years. All venues are in Lancaster.

Lancaster has a plethora of art galleries.

Annex 24 Gallery (717-341-0028), 24 West Walnut Street.

Arctic Sun Gallerie (717-341-6509), 154 North Prince St.

Artisans Gallery (717-299-9496), 114 North Prince St.

Arts Hotel Gallery (717-299-3000), 300 Harrisburg Ave.

Christiane David Gallery (717-293-0809), 112 North Prince St.

Cityfolk on Gallery Row (717-393-8807), 146 North Prince St.

D & J Scott Galleries (888-397-5360), 323 North Queen St.

Echo Valley Art Group (717-392-0606), 432 North Christian St.

Framing Concept (717-295-7290), 328 North Queen St.

Franz Fox Studios & Gallery (717-517-7053), 136 North Prince St.

Gail Gray Studio (717-393-0266), 34½ North Queen St.

Gallery 360 (717-393-1660), 24 East King St.

Gallery at DogStar Books (717-823-6605), 401 West Lemon St.

There's always something happening in downtown Lancaster.

Isadore Gallery (717-299-0127), 228 North Prince St.

J. Scott Wolf Studio & Gallery (717-271-4298), 113 North Water St.

Julia Swartz Gallery (717-397-8020; www.juliaswartz.com), 17 North Prince St.

Kalargyros & Herr Gallery (717-394-3898), 112 West Orange St.

Kathleen Abel Studio (717-393-0867), 309 East Chestnut St.

Keystone Art & Culture Center (717-870-4869), 420 Pearl St.

Lancaster Galleries (800-688-5572; www.lamcastergalleries.com), 34 North Water St.

LancasterARTS (717-509-2787; www.lancasterarts.com), 202 North Prince St, Suite 100.

Liz Hess Gallery (717-390-7222), 140 North Prince St.

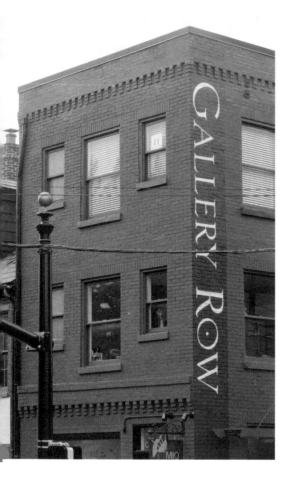

Mad-Sculptor Gallery (717-669-4924), 24 West Orange St.

Main Gallery at Pennsylvania College of Art & Design (717-396-7833; www.pcad.edu), 204 North Prince St.

Mariko Swisher Ceramics & Charles Swisher Paintings (717-397-1353), 526 Third St.

Mio Studio Gallery (717-394-6662), 154 North Prince St.

Mulberry Art Studios (717-295-1949), 19-21 North Mulberry St.

Page 4 Art Boutique (717-645-1651), 240 North Arch St.

Pariah Fine Art (570-492-1418), 113 North Water St.

Paula Egolf Studio (717-299-2522), 1010 Woods Ave.

Pennsylvania College of Art & Design (717-396-7833), 204 North Prince St.

Red Raven Art Company (717-299-4400), 138 North Prince St.

Strawberry & Co. (717-392-5345), 11 West King St.

Todd Snader's Gallery (717-397-0092; www.toddsnadersgallery.com), 27 East Lemon St.

GALLERY WALKS AND DRIVES

Contact Lancaster City Arts (120 North Duke St.; 717-291-4758) for information on its popular gallery walks and drives. The website (www.lancasterarts.com/resources/gallery-walks-and-drives.asp) offers a variety of gallery walks and drives throughout the city that will get you off the beaten path and show off the vibrant Lancaster arts community. Included are the following seven journeys:

Backstage Walk. Thirteen different sites from theaters to galleries to antiques.

Gallery Row Walk. Stroll down Lancaster's famed Gallery Row: North Prince Street.

Market Square Walk. Walk around the famed Central Market and tour a selection of distinctive galleries.

Musser Park Walk. See museums, galleries, and the Lancaster Literary Guild.

South of King Drive. Drive through some of Lancaster's most historic sections.

Uptown Walk. Jewelers, craftspeople, and artists are featured on this tour.

West End Drive. Begin at the beautiful Lancaster Arts Hotel and wind up at the Chestnut Hill Café.

Explore art in downtown Lancaster.

The website also has a downloadable map of all seven gallery walks and drives along with an additional color-coded map that corresponds to all the tours listed above.

Come visit beautiful Strasburg.

4 Towns, Burgs & Villages
SMALL-TOWN AMERICA

The small towns and distinctive villages of Lancaster County offer unique settings and equally unique experiences. Visiting these singular places can consume the better part of a vacation—a vacation filled with memories, sights, and experiences that will be remembered for many years to come.

Below are four suggested itineraries (two short, one medium, and one long), each built around a collection of towns that will provide every family member with an array of exciting experiences. You will discover some of the best Lancaster County has to offer in each of these villages along the way. Fold these routes into your travel plans and you will discover a part of America that still thrives among all the glitzy metropolises and urban behemoths.

TOUR #1—THROUGH AMISH COUNTRY

Estimated length: 29 miles
Estimated time: 1 day

Depart Lancaster City on PA-462 E. Merge onto US-30 E and travel for approximately 3 miles. Make a right turn onto PA-896 S. Travel for about 2.5 miles and you will be in the charming town of Strasburg.

STRASBURG (www.strasburgpa.com)
Strasburg today is a quaint and quiet town that caters to families. But it wasn't always so. Originally established in the early 1700s, it was an important stagecoach stop between Philadelphia and Lancaster. Taverns abounded, offering drink and cheap lodging for all sorts of itinerant travelers. For a time in the late 1700s it was quite a rowdy place—not a destination for families.

The Railroad Museum of Pennsylvania

However, as the community grew in the early 1800s it soon lost its rough edges as several schools, churches and a post office were established in town. The architecture reflected the customs and heritage of the numerous who came to the area—Germans, Swiss, and Georgians. Today, many of those 19th-century buildings (including B&Bs, historic inns and taverns, charming shops, and distinctive cafes) are sprinkled throughout the town (certainly an opportunity to get lost along the several roads through town).

FAST FACT: Some of the first settlers in the Strasburg area were French émigrés in the late 1600s.

Today, Strasburg is perhaps best known as a railroad center with all sorts of railroad attractions available for every member of the family. These include the always-popular Strasburg Railroad (the oldest short-line railroad in the United States), the Railroad Museum of Pennsylvania (more than 100 classic rail cars on display), the Choo-Choo Barn (1,700 square feet of custom model train displays), the National Toy Train Museum (an interactive collection of toy trains), and the popular Red Caboose Motel & Restaurant (you can actually sleep in a refurbished rail car).

To see:

- ❖ Strasburg Railroad
- ❖ Special Strasburg Railroad events (throughout the year)
- ❖ Railroad Museum of Pennsylvania
- ❖ Special Railroad Museum of Pennsylvania events (throughout the year)
- ❖ Choo-Choo Barn
- ❖ National Toy Train Museum
- ❖ Whoopie Pie Festival (September)
- ❖ Amish Farm and House
- ❖ Cherry Crest Adventure Farm

Depart Strasburg on PA-896 N/Hartman Bridge Road. Drive for 3.6 miles. Turn right onto PA-340 E/Old Philadelphia Pike and drive for nearly a mile. You're now in the classic Amish town of Bird-in-Hand.

BIRD-IN-HAND (www.bird-in-hand.com)

Interestingly, this town got its most unusual name as a result of a sign. In the 1700s, when the village was first established, it served as a rest stop for travelers heading west. It was also a place where local farmers met to share stories or sell their crops.

Located in the town was an inn with an elaborately painted sign out front. The sign (by an unknown artist) depicted a man holding a bird in his hand. As was the custom in the day, many places of business were denoted by painted signs, since pictures could be understood by almost all people irrespective of their nationality or level of education.

FAST FACT: Bird-in-Hand was a stop on the Underground Railroad. At least 1,000 former slaves passed through.

Apparently, folks were so entranced by the sign of the bird in the hand of a man that they decided that the name of the town should be (most appropriately) Bird-in-Hand. Walk around and you'll discover a town overflowing with quaint shops, farmer's markets, old-fashioned hardware stores, mouth-watering bakeries, and delightful restaurants. Tucked into the heart of Pennsylvania Dutch country, this market town offers visitors all sorts of wares, goodies, and apparel.

To see:

- ❖ Bird-in-Hand HomeTowne Heritage days (June)
- ❖ Amish Experience Theater
- ❖ Bird-in-Hand Farmer's Market
- ❖ Bird-in-Hand Family Restaurant
- ❖ Waters Edge Mini-Golf
- ❖ United States Hot Air Balloon Team
- ❖ Bird-in-Hand Petting Zoo

Depart Bird-in-Hand and head east on PA-340 E/Old Philadelphia Pike. After about 4 miles you will be in the vibrant village of Intercourse.

The Old Village Store in Bird-in-Hand

INTERCOURSE (www.intercoursevillage.com)

As the story goes, the village, which was originally founded in 1754, was at the intersection of two important roads—the Old King's Highway from Philadelphia to Pittsburgh (now the Old Philadelphia Pike) and the road from Wilmington, Delaware, to Erie. The intersection of these two roads is claimed by some to be the basis for the town "Cross Keys." Eventually, the name was officially changed to its synonym "Intercourse" in 1814—a name that has been postmarked on millions of outbound postcards ever since.

> **FAST FACT:** In the 18th and 19th centuries, the word "intercourse" was commonly used to describe the "fellowship" and "social interaction and support" shared in a community of faith.

The town's current claim to fame is that selected portions of the Harrison Ford movie *Witness* (1985) were filmed here. These included the phone booth scene on the porch of Zimmerman's grocery store, the fight scene on Queen Road, and the local police office (filmed in the former township building, now Peaceful Valley Amish Furniture).

Intercourse offers an interesting congregation of restaurants, services, carriage rides, tours, attractions, museums, lodging, and other businesses perfect for a peaceful stroll around town or a quiet interlude in a busy travel schedule.

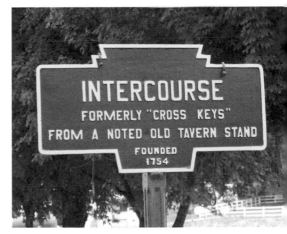

To see:

- ❖ Intercourse Fire Company Pig Roast Dinner (July)
- ❖ Lapps Coach Shop
- ❖ Intercourse Pretzel Factory
- ❖ Kitchen Kettle Village
- ❖ Historic Walking Tour of Intercourse

- ❖ The Amish Experience

- ❖ Intercourse Canning Company

- ❖ The Good Cooking Store

- ❖ The Old Country Store

Depart Intercourse and head west on PA-340 W/Old Philadelphia Pike. Drive for approximately 10 miles until you arrive in downtown Lancaster.

TOUR #2—ON THE WESTERN FRONTIER

Estimated length: 50 miles

Estimated time: 1–2 days

Depart downtown Lancaster on the Harrisburg Pike/Harrisburg Ave. Drive for 2.1 miles and turn left to merge onto US-30 W. Drive 9.3 miles and take the PA-441 exit toward Columbia/Marietta. At the end of the exit ramp, turn left onto North 3rd Street, cross over the overpass, and you will be in the town of Columbia.

COLUMBIA (www.columbiapa.net/hello-world)

Columbia was founded in 1728 and originally known as Wright's Ferry. It was John Wright, a Quaker, who in 1730 built a ferry that transported people and goods across the Susquehanna River. The Wright's Ferry Mansion, where he lived, is still located at 2nd and Cherry Streets in town.

As a major transportation hub, Columbia was a terminus for land, rail, and river routes to many destinations in the frontier of the 18th century. Later, the town was transformed into an industrial hub—supporting a wide variety of lumber, coal and

> **FAST FACT:** At one time, Columbia was under consideration as America's capital city.

Columbia has several architectural delights.

manufacturing enterprises. Many of the 18th- and 19th-century factories, man-ufacturing centers and businesses are still standing along the city's tree-lined streets. There is also an array of distinctive Victorian architecture, as well as an assembly of styles from the late 18th century all the way to art deco styles of the 20th century.

Columbia is a town with a most distinctive past and a vibrant future. It's definitely one town you won't want to miss on your travels through Lancaster County.

To see:

- ❖ Wright's Ferry Mansion
- ❖ National Watch and Clock Museum (a "must-see")
- ❖ Antiques, Arts and Crafts Show (June)
- ❖ Columbia Museum of History

- ❖ Annual Bridge Bust (October)

- ❖ Columbia Historic Market House

- ❖ First National Bank Museum

- ❖ Turkey Hill Experience

Depart Columbia and head northwest on PA-441 N/N. 3rd Street. Drive for 2.7 miles and make a slight left onto East Market St. Drive for another mile and you will be in the downtown area of Marietta.

MARIETTA (www.boroughofmarietta.com)

Marietta began in the early 1700s as a trading outpost on the American frontier. James Anderson, who operated a river-crossing site here, originally named it Anderson's Ferry. However, it was Scotch-Irish immigrants who saw the strategic location of this settlement and brought together four separate settlements in the area to create Marietta, which was officially chartered in 1812. Business and commercial enterprises sprang up, often overnight, along this stretch of river, accelerating its growth and development.

During the early 1800s, Marietta was a processing center for timber floated down the Susquehanna River from the center of the state. With the advent of the Pennsylvania Canal between 1825 and 1830, more businesses and entrepreneurs established themselves in the area to take advantage of the increased water and people traffic.

Iron was king in Marietta in the late 1900s. At one time there were at least eight separate iron furnaces east of Marietta. With all the wealth being generated from both the lumber and iron industries, it wasn't long before a string of opulent mansions began to spring up throughout the town. However, as the lumber and iron industries began to

Shank's Tavern in Marietta

FAST FACT: Marietta was formed by an alliance of four separate settlements—Waterford, New Haven, Moravian Town, and Irishtown.

Marietta is an old river town.

wane around the turn of the century, the economic energy that drove this town began to dissipate. It is now a river dowager, but one that still retains its classic lines, its 19th-century charm and a unique personality that continues to draw visitors well into the 21st century.

To see:

- ✦ Old Town Hall Museum
- ✦ Shank's Tavern
- ✦ Pig Iron Fest (late September)
- ✦ Marietta Garden Tour (June)

- ❖ Marietta Day (May)

- ❖ Candlelight Tour (early December)

- ❖ Chickies Rock Overlook

Depart Marietta on North Waterford Avenue. After crossing over PA-441, North Waterford Avenue becomes PA-772 E/Anderson Ferry Road. Continue driving for about 3.9 miles and you will arrive in the downtown area of Mount Joy.

MOUNT JOY (http://mainstreetmountjoy.com)

Mount Joy was originally founded in 1721 by Scotch-Irish immigrants and named for an Irish supply ship. Located along bustling PA-230 (once the only road that linked Lancaster and Harrisburg), the early town was an important stop for those traveling between the two cities. As a result, most of the early businesses were taverns, wagon makers, inns, and blacksmith shops.

Over time, however, the rolling countryside surrounding the town was discovered to be rich agricultural land. As a result, farming soon dominated much of the activity in and around Mount Joy. Nevertheless, much of the early architecture of this village has been lovingly restored and preserved for future generations. Walk the streets of Mount Joy and you'll get a glimpse into the past as a variety of architectural styles greet you along every avenue and around every corner. This is also a good opportunity to venture into the fertile

> **F**AST FACT: Spangler's Flour Mill (on North Market Street) has been in constant operation since 1854.

Mount Joy is over 250 years old.

countryside that surrounds the town to view the many farms that dot the land-scape.

Mount Joy is a town revitalized—in fact, the state of Pennsylvania designated Mount Joy as a "Main Street Community" in 2002. As a visitor, you'll have several unique opportunities to step back into the past while enjoying an abundance of current events, activities, and lively festivals.

To see:

- ❖ Small Town Murals Trail

- ❖ Fourth Fridays in downtown Mount Joy (4th Friday of every month)

- ❖ Taste of Mount Joy—Cruisin' Cuisine (July)

- ❖ Crabfest (September)

- ❖ Winterfest (December)

- ❖ Bube's Brewery

- ❖ Music in the Park (June, July, August)

- ❖ Farmer's Market

Depart Mount Joy on PA-230 W/W. Main St. Continue on PA-230 W for approx-imately 6.3 miles and you will be in the charming village of Elizabethtown.

ELIZABETHTOWN (www.etownonline.net)

Known as "E-town" to locals, Elizabethtown was originally settled by Scotch-Irish immigrants. One Brabas Hughes acquired some land here and turned the local trading post into one of the largest anywhere between Philadelphia and Pittsburgh. By 1753 Brabas had laid out the town and named it after his wife. With the onslaught of the French and Indian War, the Revolu-tionary War and the War of 1812, de-velopment in the town languished. It wasn't until the arrival of the railroad in 1832 that the town began to experi-ence a resurgence in both population and popularity.

Walk the downtown area and you

Welcome to Elizabethtown.

will be immediately taken with the variety of 19th- and early 20th-century buildings.

Stroll around the square at the intersection of High and Market streets and
you can almost feel the history oozing out of every structure. The town's charm
is enhanced with an eclectic variety of shops, galleries, museums, and cafes. Be
sure to look up at the colorful paintings adorning the sides of various buildings
throughout the town.

Elizabethtown is a destination for all who appreciate a vibrant downtown
area, an emphasis on historic preservation, and a celebration of both past and
present. Make sure it's on your itinerary.

To see:

   ✤ Arts in the Park (mid-May)

   ✤ Summer Lunch Series on the Square (late May through July)

❖ Elizabethtown Fair

❖ Winters Heritage House Museum

❖ Samuel S. Haldeman Mansion

❖ Scotch-Irish Festival (May)

❖ Bellaire Woods-Lancaster County Conservancy

❖ Conewago Trail

> **F**AST FACT: In the early 20th century, the tuition at Elizabethtown College was $1 per week.

Depart Elizabethtown on PA-230 E/S. Market St. Travel for about 2.7 miles and make a left turn onto Cloverleaf Road. Drive for almost a mile and take the PA-283 E ramp to Lancaster. Drive for another 12.4 miles and take the PA-72/Manheim Pike exit. Keep right at the fork and follow the signs for downtown Lancaster.

TOUR #3—OLD TIME LANCASTER COUNTY

Estimated length: 25 miles

Estimated time: Half day

Depart downtown Lancaster on US-222 N (also known as PA-272 N and the Lititz Pike). After you travel under US-30 the road changes over to PA-501 N (it's still known as Lititz Pike). Follow PA-501 N for about 7 miles and you will arrive in Lititz.

LITITZ (www.lititzpa.com)

Don't miss Lititz! The town recently won an online poll at BudgetTravel.com as "the Coolest Small Town in the Country." Now who wouldn't want to visit this energetic village nestled in north-central Lancaster County?

In so many ways, Lititz has it all. History, architecture, shops, parks, festivals, restaurants . . . everything you would want to see in small-town America. This is one place you definitely want to include on your travels throughout Lancaster County. If you can't find it here, then it probably doesn't exist.

Long before the arrival of European settlers, this vibrant landscape was inhabited by the Nanticoke Indians. It wasn't until 1722 that the first

> **F**AST FACT: Linden Hall School, an independent school for girls in Lititz, was founded in 1746. It is the oldest girls' boarding/day school in the country.

Linden Hall School in Lititz

settler, Christian Bomberger built and lived in the first house in the area. In 1749 Moravians, who were seeking religious freedom and tolerance in the New World, began to establish a network of farms in the region. For nearly 100 years the area was almost exclusively settled by Moravians who were more interested in preserving their religious beliefs than in starting a new town.

However, in the 1850s the religious code could not be sustained and non-Moravians were given permission to settle in the area. As you walk around town you can still see the Moravian influence in the form of Moravian stars hanging from storefronts, churches, window balconies, and homes.

What you will also notice is a rich mixture of German, English, and Victorian influences in the architecture of the town. There is a variety of homes with quite interesting facades—log, brick, stone—that reflect the different cultural influences that have played a part in the long history of this village. The town is able to combine its history with its past, showcasing a dynamic assortment of

Lititz, the coolest small town in the country

cafes, inns, shops, restaurants, B&Bs, galleries, and other establishments that will invite you to stay for more than just a casual visit.

To see:

- ❖ Fire and Ice Festival (February)
- ❖ Teddy Bear Day in the Park (September)
- ❖ Lititz Chocolate Walk (October)
- ❖ Moravian Church Square
- ❖ Historic Lititz Guided Walking Tour
- ❖ Wilbur Chocolate Factory
- ❖ Downtown Lititz Saturday Farmer's Market
- ❖ Annual Lititz Outdoor Art Show (July)
- ❖ Annual Fall Antique Show (August)
- ❖ Lititz Spring Park

Manheim has lots to offer.

Depart Lititz on PA-772 W/W. Orange St. Continue to follow PA-772 W (it turns into Temperance Hill Road and then Fruitville Pike) for 4.8 miles. Make a right turn onto South Main Street and travel for about half a mile and you will be in Manheim.

MANHEIM (www.manheimdowntown.org)

Manheim was named by the flamboyant Henrich Wilhelm Stiegel. He often traveled in a four-horse carriage and whenever he approached his home on Market Square, a watchman sounded a cannon and a band played music to signal his arrival. According to legend, Stiegel named the town for the area of Germany in

> **F**AST FACT: Manheim is home to the world's largest auto auction. It's open for business every Friday.

which he was raised. It was his hope that the new Manheim would become a cultural and industrial center.

Stiegel established a glass-making factory, which unfortunately failed in 1774. He endured a number of other financial misfortunes throughout his career, but his vision lived on in the form of numerous commercial and industrial projects. Some of these enterprises included the manufacture of grandfather clocks, bricks, and hats in addition to the establishment of several tanners, blacksmiths, wagon shops, and potters. If nothing else, the glass he produced—Stiegel glass—is still prized today as a highly desirable collectible.

The "golden age" of Manheim's commercial success was in the early part of the 19th century. When the railroad came to town in 1862, the economy took off like a rocket with access to numerous transportation routes for manufactured goods. Unfortunately, the bottom fell out of the local economy with the advent of the Depression, but the town has survived quite well in the modern era with a delightful mix of old and new.

Walk through the town and you are likely to see stately Victorian homes on the same street as log cabins. You'll discover elegant B&Bs along with quite modern hotels. You'll come upon cozy cafes as well as distinctive restaurants. In short, you'll discover a rich blend of what once was and what is now.

To see:

- ❖ Cruisin' the Square (October)
- ❖ Holiday Tree Lighting (late November)
- ❖ Mount Hope Estate and Winery
- ❖ Fasig and Keath Houses
- ❖ Manheim Railroad Station
- ❖ Manheim Heritage Center
- ❖ Annual Spring Craft and Antique Show (June)
- ❖ Manheim Call Festival Antique Car Show (October)

Depart Manheim southeast on PA-72 S/S. Main St. Follow PA-72 S for 10.5 miles and you will arrive back in downtown Lancaster.

TOUR #4—RELIGION AND ANTIQUES

Estimated length: 50 miles

Estimated time: Half a day–1 day

Depart Lancaster on PA-272 N/US-222 N. After about 1.5 miles, make a slight right onto PA-272 N/US-222 N/Oregon Pike. Drive for half a mile and take the ramp onto US-222N/US-30 E. Keep right to continue onto US-222 N. Travel for about 10.5 miles on US-222 N and take the US-322 exit toward Ephrata. Turn left onto US-322 W/E. Main St. After 2 miles you will arrive in Ephrata.

EPHRATA (www.ephrataboro.org)

The centerpiece of this town—and the reason so many people journey here—is the well-known Ephrata Cloister. The founder of Ephrata Cloister, Conrad Beissel, was born in Germany in 1691. As a young man he encountered Pietism, a movement to reform the state-sanctioned Protestant churches. However, as a

The Ephrata Cloister in Ephrata

The Ephrata Cloister

Pietist, Beissel was found to be in conflict with the church. He was ultimately banished from his homeland and eventually immigrated to Pennsylvania in 1720.

Beissel eventually found his way to an area just east of present-day Lancaster and affiliated himself with the Brethren, an Anabaptist group. In 1724 he was appointed leader of the newly formed Conestoga Brethren Congregation. Beissel had some radical ideas for the group, including Saturday worship and celibacy. In 1732 he broke away from the group and, along with several followers, established a site along the banks of the Cocalico Creek in northern Lancaster County—now known as Ephrata Cloister.

> **F**AST FACT: Ephrata is named after Ephrath, a biblical town in what is now Israel.

What began as a hermitage for a small group of devoted individuals grew into a thriving community of nearly 80 celibate members supported by an estimated 200 family members from the region at its zenith in the mid-18th century. The community became known for its self-composed a cappella music, Germanic calligraphy known as *Frakturschriften,* and a complete publishing center which included a paper mill, printing office, and book bindery.

Today, this National Historic Landmark is administered by the Pennsylvania Historical and Museum Commission. Daily tours, special programs, and ongoing research continue to inform and educate visitors about Ephrata's surviving legacy and the people who built it.

To see:

- ❖ Ephrata Cloister
- ❖ Apple Dumpling Days at Ephrata Cloister (October)
- ❖ Lantern Tours at Ephrata Cloister (December)
- ❖ Historical Society of Cocalico Valley
- ❖ Ephrata Street Fair (September)
- ❖ William Penn Heritage Day (October)

Head northwest on West Main St. After half a mile, make a right turn onto PA-272 N/N. Reading Road. Drive for approximately 8.1 miles and you will arrive in Adamstown.

ADAMSTOWN (www.antiquescapital.com)

If there were ever two words that naturally went together, they would be Adamstown and antiques. Adamstown bills itself as Antiques Capital USA, and if you ever wanted to see what an entire town devoted to antiques looked like, then this is your place.

There are more than 5,000 (yes, you read that right) antique dealers here to satisfy your every craving, wish, and desire (antiques-wise that is). If it's old, then it's probably in Adamstown. You'll discover antiques shops and stores and vendors all over the place. The challenge will be in deciding on which ones to visit and which ones to skip (never an easy task).

You know you're in antique heaven when you see all the restaurants, cafes, diners, hotels, motels, B&Bs, and other attractions that serve the tens of thousands of visitors who

FAST FACT: Adamstown is home to the country's oldest hat manufacturer—the Bollman Hat Company, founded in 1868.

Adamstown is an antiques bonanza.

come here every year to stare, beg, bargain, and buy thousands of treasures of every size and shape. Whether you're looking for a tiny piece of jewelry or an enormous chunk of furniture, this is the place . . . this is the town. In fact, some folks plan their entire visit or their entire vacation around Adamstown.

To see:

- ✤ Antiques Extravaganza (late April, June, and September)
- ✤ Adamstown Antiques Gallery
- ✤ Clock Tower Antiques at Stoudtburg
- ✤ Heritage Antiques Center
- ✤ Time Matters Antique Mall
- ✤ Renninger's Antique Market
- ✤ Stoudt's Black Angus Antique Mall

Depart Adamstown and head northeast on PA-272. After about 1 mile turn right to merge onto PA-222 S toward Lancaster. Drive for about 23.3 miles and you'll be back in downtown Lancaster.

Erb's Mill Bridge

5 Covered Bridges & Scenic Drives

BACK ROADS & ROLLING HILLS

Lancaster County is ripe for exploration—here you'll discover distinctive architecture, delightful vistas, incredible stories and a panoply of culture, language, and history. This is a county overflowing with magical experiences for each and every visitor. So grab this book, jump in your car, and get ready to drive yourself happy with this collection of tours, trips, and treasures.

COVERED BRIDGES

Travel through almost any part of Lancaster County and you'll likely come across one of the most unique features on the landscape—a covered bridge. These distinctive architectural buildings are certainly not unique to Lancaster, yet they are so ubiquitous that they are frequently pictured as Lancaster County's most recognizable icons.

One of the features early settlers to this part of the country discovered upon their arrival was an abundance of swift flowing streams and rivers. Being practical people, they quickly saw not only a water source, but a source of energy that could be used to power all sorts of mills and other industries. As the mills were constructed, villages and farming communities grew up in the general vicinity. To access those communities and to take advantage of an immediate source of lumber it was necessary to cross over the numerous streams. The abundance of old growth

> **FAST FACT:** Lancaster County has 29 covered bridges—the most in any county in Pennsylvania and second most in the country (only Parke County, Indiana, with 31, has more).

Forry's Mill Bridge

lumber provided a ready resource for the construction of the bridges needed to span those waterways—a cheap and natural source of building materials.

It soon became evident that a bridge left to the elements would disintegrate very quickly. As a result, it seemed necessary that some form of protection should be used in order to protect a bridge's wooden beams and surface area. The most practical solution was the construction of walls and a roof over the bridge to ensure its longevity and preservation. The result was the covered bridge . . . or more appropriately, many covered bridges over many different waterways.

The construction of these bridges was so professional that many of them have survived for a hundred years or more. Bridges were normally constructed by local bridge builders, which is why construction styles vary throughout the county. The fact that so many of them have survived is certainly a salute to the craftsmanship of the people who built these unique structures so long ago.

COVERED BRIDGE TOUR #1—HIGHWAYS & BYWAYS

Estimated length: 27 miles
Estimated time: 1–1.5 hours

Begin your tour in the city of Lancaster. Drive west on PA-23 for about 8.3 miles. When you come to the intersection with Prospect Road, travel an additional mile on PA-23 and make a right turn onto Bridge Valley Road, and drive 0.2 mile. Ahead of you will be **Forry's Mill Bridge.** Constructed in 1869, this 102-foot structure over Chickies Creek was originally named for the Forry family who lived on the adjoining property. Located in a beautiful rural setting, it is one of many bridges throughout Lancaster County either built or repaired by Elias McMellen. Some repairs to the bridge were made in 1925.

Drive through the bridge and continue on Bridge Valley Road for 1.2 miles. At Pinkerton Road travel straight onto Longenecker Road and travel for an additional 2.2 miles. Turn left onto PA-230/East Main St. (Mount Joy). Drive for 1 mile and turn right onto PA-772 E/Manheim St. Travel for 3.3 miles and turn

Shenck's Mill Bridge

right onto Ebenshade Road. Drive for 0.8 mile and make a sharp left onto Auction Road (right before the PA-283 overpass) and drive for 1.2 miles. Turn right onto Erisman Road and proceed for 0.3 mile. You will come to **Shenck's Mill Bridge**. This bridge, constructed in 1855, is unusual in that it is one of the very few bridges in Lancaster County with horizontal siding. You will also note two long horizontal windows on the eastern end of the bridge (function: unknown). Its location in a beautiful rural setting makes it a delight to visit.

Drive through the bridge, turn around, and drive back through the bridge. Continue on Erisman Road for 0.1 mile and make a right turn at Auction Road and drive for 1.3 miles. Turn left onto Colebrook Road and drive for 1.1 miles. Turn right onto PA-772/Mount Joy Road and drive for 0.6 mile. Turn right onto Sun Hill Road. After 0.1 mile, you'll see **Kaufman's Distillery Bridge**. Built in 1874 and also known as Sporting Hill Bridge, this bridge was affiliated with a local distillery owned by the Kaufman family. According to published reports, the Kaufman family would travel throughout the county selling whiskey in various local towns such as Mount Joy, Elizabethtown, and Manheim.

Shearer's Mill Bridge

Go through the bridge, turn around, drive back through the bridge and back to PA-772/Mount Joy Road. Turn right onto PA-772 and drive for 1.1 miles. At the light in the center square of Manheim, bear slightly to the right and then proceed straight ahead. Continue to the next light and

> **F**AST FACT: At one time in Pennsylvania, there were at least 1,526 covered bridges. Today only about 200 to 220 remain—which is still more than any other state.

make a left turn onto Main Street, then turn right onto Gramby Road. Drive for 0.7 mile and turn left onto Laurel Street. Proceed for 0.1 mile and make a right turn onto Adele Avenue. After 0.3 mile you will have arrived at **Shearer's Mill Bridge**. This bridge is very similar in design to Shenck's Mill Bridge in that the siding is horizontal and there are two long horizontal windows on one end of the bridge. It was originally constructed in 1856 (for $600) over Chickies Creek; then in 1971 it was moved 4 miles to Manheim Memorial Park and rebuilt.

After this tour, you will find yourself in the quaint Lancaster County town of Manheim. Check out some of the sites and scenes of this town (see Chapter 4), including some of its distinctive restaurants.

COVERED BRIDGE TOUR #2—AMISH COUNTRYSIDE

Estimated length: 20 miles

Estimated time: 1.5 hours

Start this tour in Lancaster City. Get onto PA-23 E. As you pass over US-30, glance at your odometer. Then continue on PA-23 E for 2.4 miles and make a left turn onto Mondale Road. Travel for 0.3 mile and turn left onto Hunsecker Road. Travel for 0.2 mile and you'll arrive at **Hunsecker's Mill Bridge**. The setting for this bridge is stunning. The bridge was originally built in 1843. However, in the intervening years it has been swept off its abutments several times due to flooding. In 1972 Hurricane Agnes completely destroyed the bridge, but local citizens ensured its rebuilding to the tune of $321,000 (it took two years to restore).

Continue through Hunsecker's Bridge and travel for an additional 0.6 mile. Make a right turn onto Butter Road and drive for 1.2 miles. Make a right turn onto Bridge Road (at the one-lane bridge sign), and you will come to **Pinetown Covered Bridge**. Originally constructed in 1867, this 133-foot structure across

Hunsecker's Mill Bridge

the Conestoga River has been beaten and battered by numerous storms over the years. It was heavily damaged by Hurricane Agnes in 1972 and then again by Tropical Storm Lee in 2011. It was closed in 2011 and extensively repaired in 2013. The bridge originally cost $4,500 to build just after the Civil War; its 2013 reconstruction came in at a whopping $818,546.

After viewing the Pinetown Bridge, continue on the previous road (don't cross the bridge). The road changes its name to Pinetown Road (Bridge Road continues across the river). Drive for 0.4 mile then make a left turn onto Bushong Road and drive for 0.4 mile. Make a right turn onto PA-272 and drive for 0.8 mile. Turn left onto Rose Hill Road and continue for half a mile. Make a left turn onto Log Cabin Road and drive to **Zook's Mill Bridge**. As with many other bridges in

Lancaster County, this one is known by other names, including Wenger's Bridge, Rose Hill Bridge, and Cocalico 7 Bridge. Constructed in 1849, it is one of the county's oldest bridges. After Hurricane Agnes in 1972 (look for the water level sign inside the structure), the horizontal siding on this bridge was replaced with vertical siding.

Inside Zook's Mill Bridge

Interestingly, the load limit for this bridge is about 7 tons (most covered bridges, particularly if steel reinforcements have not been added, can only carry between 2 and 5 tons).

Continue through the bridge for an additional 1 mile. Turn right onto Church Road and drive for 1.1 miles. Make a right turn onto PA-772/Main Street and proceed for half a mile. Turn left at the traffic signal onto Rothsville Road and drive for 1.1 miles. Make a left turn on Middle Creek Road and drive for half a mile to **Keller's Mill Bridge**. Known by most of the locals as Guy Bard's Bridge (Guy Bard was a leading Pennsylvania jurist who lived in the area), it has also been called Cocalico 5 Bridge and Rettews Bridge. This bridge stands out from all the other Lancaster County bridges as the only remaining white one in the county. When it was first constructed in 1891 it was a short distance away on Rettew Mill Road. It was moved to its present location in 2010.

Continue through the bridge on Middle Creek Road for almost a mile. You will then cross over Meadow Valley Road (be careful—there are blind curves in both directions). Stay on Middle Creek Road and just before you make the next turn you'll notice a one-room Amish schoolhouse on your left. Then turn left on Erb's Bridge Road and drive for half a mile to **Erb's Mill Bridge**. Also known as Hammer 1 Bridge, this structure spans Hammer Creek and was built in 1887. The bridge was originally named for the Erb family, who lived nearby. It is in a beautiful location and its construction (vertical boards, stone and mortar wingwalls, barn red color) are typical of many Lancaster County bridges.

After viewing this final bridge on the tour, continue driving on Erb's Bridge Road (it turns into Picnic Woods Road) for 1.4 miles. Make a right turn onto PA 772/Main Street and drive for 0.2 mile. Bear left onto PA-772/Rothsville Road

Keller's Mill Bridge

and journey into the delightful and charming town of Lititz (see Chapter 4). This is a great place to end your journey, visit some of the shops, and enjoy a fabulous midday meal.

COVERED BRIDGE TOUR #3—RURAL ROADS

Estimated length: 30 miles
Estimated time: 2 hours

This journey will take you through some of the most beautiful rural countryside in all of Lancaster County. Start your tour in the classic town of Strasburg (see Chapter 4). After you've ridden the Strasburg Railroad or visited the Railroad Museum, hop in your car and drive west on PA-741/Main Street for about 1.5 miles.

Make sure you stay on PA-741 as it bears to the left at a Y intersection, and then to the right. When you get to Penn Grant Road, make a left turn and drive for 0.2 mile. Turn right at the stop sign onto Hagers/Penn Grant Road and proceed for 1.2 miles. You'll arrive at **Neff's Mill Bridge**. Known also as the Pequea 7 Bridge, this structure was erected in 1875 over Pequea Creek. According to some reports, this bridge may be one of the narrowest covered bridges in Lancaster County. With a total width of 12 feet, 10 inches it does limit the types of vehicles that can safely travel through. It is distinguished by a small window on both the left and right side.

Continue on Penn Grant Road for 0.2 mile and turn left onto Pequea Lane. Drive for 1.1 miles and make a right turn at the stop sign onto Lime Valley Road. Drive for 0.3 mile and turn left onto Brenneman Road. You will be at **Lime Valley Bridge**. Originally built in 1871 over Pequea Creek, this is one of the few Lancaster County bridges that survived virtually intact after Hurricane Agnes in 1972. Also known as the Pequea 8 Bridge and the Strasburg Bridge, it is distinguished by long wingwalls and parapets and is supported on stone and mortar abutments. It is an ideal bridge to walk or drive through.

Continue driving on Brenneman Road for 0.9 mile. Cross over US-222, bearing right onto Main Street (look for the sign), and drive for 0.3 mile. Make a left turn onto Refton Road and continue for 0.3 mile. Turn right onto Smithville Road and drive for almost a mile. When you come to a Y intersection, bear right on Byerland Church Road and drive for 0.4 mile. Make a left turn onto PA-272 and proceed for 0.8 mile. Turn right onto Pennsy Road and drive for 3.3 miles (you will cross over Rawlinsville Road). Pennsy Road will change over into Highway 324 at an intersection with a stop sign. Continue on Highway 324 for 2 more miles. Make a sharp left turn onto Fox Hollow Road (there will be a sign: Pequea Creek Campground) and drive for 0.2 mile. You'll be at **Colemanville Bridge**. Also known as Martic Forge Bridge, it was built in 1856 and stands as one of the longest bridges (167 feet, 7 inches) in Lancaster County. As with several bridges in the county it has over the years been subjected to several floods and was repaired and upgraded in both 1973 (after Hurricane Agnes) and 1991. You'll want to stroll through this dynamic and imposing structure.

After viewing the bridge, turn

> **F**AST FACT: Covered bridges are also known as "kissing bridges." Tradition holds that if you kiss your sweetheart while traveling through a covered bridge you will have good luck.

Lime Valley Bridge

your car around and return to Highway 324. Make a right turn and drive for 2 miles. Make a left at the Y intersection and follow Marticville Road for 1.1 miles. Make a right turn onto Frogtown Road and drive for half a mile. Make a left turn when you see the sign for the covered bridge (this is Covered Bridge Road.). You'll arrive at **Baumgardener's Bridge**. This bridge (also known as Pequea 10 Bridge) was originally constructed in 1860 and spans Pequea Creek. It was reconstructed in 1987; you'll notice the extensive improvements made in this structure to ensure that it lasts another century or more. This bridge is almost 116 feet in length and offers some good photo opportunities.

Continue through the bridge (on Covered Bridge Road) for 0.7 mile. Make a left turn at Mount Hope School Road and travel for 0.7 mile. Make a left turn at the T intersection (there's no street sign—but it's Rawlinsville Road), and drive for 1 mile. Make a right turn onto Baumgardener Road and drive for 0.7 mile. Turn right onto PA-272/Willow Street and then move over to the left lane as quickly as you can. At the first median turn-off, make a left turn to travel north on PA-272 for 1.6 miles. Make a right turn at the traffic signal at Beaver Valley Road and drive for 0.2 mile. Turn left onto Eshlemen Mill Road and drive for 2.3 miles. Turn left onto Golf Road and drive for 0.2 mile. Make a left onto Kiwanis Road and drive for 0.2 mile. You will be at **Kurtz's Mill Bridge**. This bridge may have an identity crisis—since it is also known by three other names: Baer's Mill Bridge, Isaac Bean's Mill Bridge, and Keystone Mill Bridge. It also has been re-located approximately 15 miles from its original location—it's now crossing Mill Creek inside Lancaster Central County Park. When it was built in 1876, it cost $1,407; when it was reconstructed in 1973 (after Hurricane Agnes) the cost of restoration was $55,000.

After viewing the bridge, turn around and follow Kiwanis Road back to Golf

Kurtz's Mill Bridge

Road. Make a left turn onto Golf Road and drive for 1.4 miles. When you come to US-222/Queen Street, make a right turn and travel into downtown Lancaster.

COVERED BRIDGE TOUR #4— NORTHERN LANCASTER COUNTY

Estimated length: 32 miles
Estimated time: 1.5–2 hours

This tour begins and ends in the historic town of Ephrata (see Chapter 4). You may wish to take an entire day to visit the Ephrata Cloister, tour some covered bridges, and partake of all the other historical offerings in this classic Lancaster County town. You'll begin your journey at the intersection of PA-322 and PA-272. From here, head north on PA-272 for 3 miles. Make a right turn onto Cocalico Creek Road (careful—the street sign is small and comes up quite quickly). Travel for 0.3 mile and you'll arrive at **Bucher's Mill Bridge**. Constructed in 1892, this bridge has also been known as Cocalico 2 Bridge. It was immediately destroyed one year after it was built, but rebuilt immediately. It survived quite well over the years and was refurbished in both 1966 and 1997. As with many Lancaster County bridges it is in a picturesque location (over Cocalico Creek).

Drive through the bridge and continue on Cocalico Creek Road for 0.1 mile. Make a right turn onto Creek Lane (there's no street sign) and drive for 0.3 mile. Make a left turn onto Reamstown Road and drive for 0.6 mile. Turn right onto East Church Street and continue for 1.6 miles. Make a left turn onto Red Run Road and drive for 1.9 miles. Turn left onto Martin Church Road and you'll see **Red Run Bridge**. Unfortunately, you won't be able to drive through this bridge, which is experiencing some degree of deterioration. Originally built in 1866, it was bypassed in 1961 with the construction of a new bridge. It has been variously used as a church, a storage area, and a source of lumber to refurbish wagons.

After viewing Red Run Bridge, return to Red Run Road. Make a left turn and the road quickly makes a sharp turn to the left (don't assume the road goes straight ahead). Continue on Red Run Road for another 1.7 miles. Make a right turn onto Maple Street and travel for 0.2 mile. Turn left onto West Main Street and drive for 3.8 miles. You'll go through the intersec-

> **FAST FACT:** At one time, 64 of Pennsylvania's 67 counties had at least one covered bridge in use.

Red Run Bridge

tion of Reading Road and Highway 625. The road will now change names—first into Union Grove Road and then into Churchtown Road. Make a right turn at Weaverland Road and drive for 0.6 mile. You'll come to **Weaver's Mill Bridge**. This 88-foot long bridge spans Conestoga Creek. Built in 1878, it is also known as Isaac Shearer's Mill Bridge. Depending on the day and time you visit, you may see Amish horses and buggies driving through this structure on a regular basis.

After viewing the bridge, return to Churchtown Road. Turn right onto Churchtown Road and travel for 1 mile. Make a right onto Pool Forge Road and drive for 0.2 mile. Turn right onto PA-23/Main Street and then make a quick left onto Pool Forge Road. After about 0.1 mile, look to your left and you will see **Pool**

Bitzer's Mill Bridge

Forge Bridge. This bridge, constructed in 1859, is no longer open to vehicular traffic (it is now privately owned). Spanning the Conestoga Creek it is 99 feet, 3 inches long and 15 feet, 6 inches wide. As with many Lancaster County bridges, it has vertical siding and stone and mortar wingwalls. The bridge is significant because this was reportedly the place where President James Buchanan met his fiancé (unfortunately, she died before they could marry).

After viewing the bridge, return to PA-23/Main Street. Make a left turn onto PA-23 and drive for 4 miles. When you come to the intersection with PA-

322, make a right turn onto PA-322 and drive for an additional 4.3 miles. Make a left turn onto Farmersville Road and proceed for 0.3 mile. Turn right onto Goods Drive and travel for nearly a mile. Turn right onto Goods Road. When you come to the stop sign, bear right onto Cats Back Road. Ahead will be **Bitzer's Mill Bridge**.

> **F**AST FACT: The longest covered bridge in the world spanned the mile-wide Susquehanna River between Columbia and Wrightsville, Pennsylvania. It was 5,960 feet in length.

Also known as Eberly's Cider Mill Bridge, this bridge was constructed in 1846. It is reported to be the oldest state-owned bridge in Pennsylvania. Carved into one of its arches is the following—"ETERNITY! Where will you spend it? Your choice. Heaven or Hell." That proclamation is ironic, given that this bridge has been the object of several arsons over the years.

Continue through the bridge on Cats Back Road for 0.4 mile (note that the road changes its name to Cider Mill Road). When you come to the Y intersection, make a right turn onto Willis Pierce Road and drive for 0.2 mile. Make a left turn onto Pleasant Valley Road and drive for 1.4 miles. Make a left onto PA-322 and drive for about 2 miles back into the downtown area of Ephrata.

SCENIC DRIVES

Power up your camera or cell phone because you're in for some visual delights— scenic trips that many Lancaster County visitors miss. The following tours will dazzle you and delight you with an array of rural wonders. You'll view Amish farms, rolling countryside, long rows of corn, and a world totally unlike anything you may have at home. These tours will help you appreciate all that Lancaster County has to offer and everything that will help make your journey here complete.

These tours have been designed so they can be easily tucked into other Lancaster County activities. You'll be able to easily add one or more of these trips to all the other plans on your itinerary. Also, these tours don't appear in any of the tourist information you're likely to collect during your visit here, so they can be an added bonus to the places and attractions that brought you here in the first place. Above all, you'll get a better sense of this vibrant county and the reasons why it was so attractive to early settlers (Native Americans *and* Europeans) a few hundred years ago.

SCENIC TOUR # 1—PHOTOGRAPHIC OPPORTUNITIES

Estimated length: 40 miles

Estimated time: 1.5–2 hours

Begin this tour on US-30 E. The first thing you notice is the jumble and onslaught of stores, shopping malls, fast-food restaurants, chain establishments, outlet stores, and other assorted commercial enterprises.

After passing the intersection of PA-896, US-30 becomes a little more civilized—that is, the malls and shopping centers tend to disappear, and the farms and farmhouses make an appearance alongside the road. Soon you'll arrive in Paradise (the town, that is). Continue on US-30 and travel through the traffic signal at PA-772. At the traffic signal in Gap, make a right turn on PA-41. Continue through the next traffic light (notice the clock tower on the left side). Travel for an additional 2.4 miles and bear right onto Newport Road (look for the small brown sign: "Welcome to Christiana, Pennsylvania").

Continue on to the stop sign. Go straight through the intersection (look for

Historic Zercher's Hotel

the "Welcome to Christiana" sign on your left). Continue straight ahead. Bear right at Pine Street (look for small sign on post: Business District). Bear right at Elizabeth Street. Make a left turn onto Green Street. At the

> **F**AST FACT: Christiana is the least populous borough (population: 1,124) in Lancaster County.

corner of Green and E. Slokom Avenue (on your left) will be the Cristiana Underground Railroad Center at Historic Zercher Hotel.

The Zercher hotel may appear unassuming, yet its place in history is anything but. For many, the hotel, and the events it harbored, remains as one of the most significant catalysts to spark the Civil War. As you will discover when you stop in, this unassuming site holds enormous historical significance. It was here in 1851 that four white men and 37 African Americans were arrested for treason (the largest number of Americans to be charged with treason in this country's history) for challenging, and breaking, the Fugitive Slave Law. Although they were all eventually acquitted, their actions are often cited as one of the major catalysts for the Civil War.

After viewing the tiny museum, gaze at the stone monument just outside, and revel in how a small band of determined individuals can ignite a mighty fire.

From here, continue straight ahead on Green Street to the stop sign and make a right turn on Branch Street (going under the overpass). Bear right at the Y, then bear left onto W. Slokom Avenue, and you'll come to a stop sign (North Bridge Street). Make a left turn onto Bridge Street. At the stop sign, make a right turn onto Water Street. After 0.2 mile, bear right onto Germantown Avenue.

You will have exited the town of Christiana and will now find yourself in some very beautiful countryside—wide farms, rolling hills, clumps of trees, cornfields—all typical rural Pennsylvania. You'll also pass between several dairy farms and their ever-present guardians—the cows (who love to have their picture taken, by the way).

You'll next come to the intersection of PA-896 S and PA-372 S. Make a left turn onto PA-372 S (notice the stream on your right side). Drive for 1 mile and you'll arrive at a blinking signal. Make a right turn onto PA-372 W. Travel for 3.2 miles and make a right onto May Post Office Road. This road travels through some of the most beautiful scenery you're likely to see in Lancaster County— fields of corn, lots of barns, Amish farms, and clumps of trees. Make sure you have your camera ready.

You'll have lots of bovine company on your drives through Lancaster County.

After 6.5 miles on May Post Office Road, you'll arrive at the intersection of PA-741 and May Post Office Road in the railroad town Strasburg. Make a left turn onto PA-741 W at the traffic signal. After 0.4 mile you'll come to a Y in the road. Bear right onto Lancaster Avenue (also known as Strasburg Pike). Drive for 4.9 miles and you will arrive at the intersection of Strasburg Pike and PA-462. Make a left turn onto PA-462 and return to the city of Lancaster.

SCENIC DRIVE #2—SEVERAL PROMINENT PEOPLE

Estimated length: 75 miles
Estimated time: Half a day to 1 day

This drive will take you along some highways and byways to discover some of the movers and shakers that once lived in Lancaster County. Along the way, you'll discover some of the amazing history of this part of the country along with the stories of some fascinating individuals.

From Lancaster, head south on PA-222 (South Prince Street). Turn left on Seymour Street, drive for a short distance and then make a left on PA-222 N. After a short distance make a right onto Chesapeake Street. Follow Chesapeake Street for about 1 mile, then make a right turn onto East Strawberry Street. Look for the sign indicating the **Rock Ford Plantation**.

Standing on the wooded banks of the Conestoga River, this Georgian-style brick mansion (built circa-1794) is a remarkably preserved remnant of 18th century living. It was the colonial estate of Edward Hand (1744-1802), who rose to become Adjutant General to George Washington in 1781.

Rock Ford is an excellent example of refined country living, particularly

Rock Ford Plantation

FAST FACT: Robert Fulton was one of the most accomplished artists of his time. His miniature portraits are considered to be some of the finest ever produced in this country.

during the 18th century. The four floors of this house remain exactly as they were when Hand and his family lived here more than two centuries ago. As you walk through the house (all tours are self-guided) you will notice the meticulously furnished rooms with period antiques and original artifacts belonging to the Hand family. You'll want to pay particular attention to the original rails, shutters, doors, cupboards, paneling, and window panes.

After departing Rock Ford, direct your car over to US-222 S. Drive south until you come to the town of Willow Street. Just north of town, US-222 changes over to PA-272. Stay on US-222 (it diverges sharply to the left at a traffic signal) and continue your journey south. You are headed through the towns of New Providence and Quarryville to the **Robert Fulton Birthplace**, which is located just before US-222 intersects again with PA-272 in southern Lancaster County. The driving distance from Rock Ford to Fulton's birthplace is about 20.1 miles and will take about 30 minutes.

Robert Fulton is probably best remembered for having built the steamboat Clermont which, in 1807, successfully navigated the Hudson River. He is incorrectly remembered (at least in some history books) as the inventor of the steamship.

Visit this small but charming house and you too will be taken back to another era. You'll be able to see what life was like in the mid-1700s. This home looks much the way it did when Fulton was a child—the simplicity of the furnishings and the furniture are testament to the simplicity of life in 18th-century Lancaster County.

After departing the Robert Fulton Birthplace, turn right out of the driveway and continue heading south on US-222. You will quickly come to the intersection with PA-272. Make another right turn and head north on PA-272. Continue up PA-272 until you get back to the city of Lancaster. Drive through Penn Square and make a left turn onto Orange Street. Travel on Orange Street until you come to its intersection with PA-23 (also known as Marietta Avenue). Turn right and proceed for about 0.7 mile until you arrive at **James Buchanan's Wheatland** on the left side of the road. The driving distance from the Robert Fulton Birthplace to Wheatland is about 23.1 miles and will take you approximately 35 minutes.

Robert Fulton Birthplace

While he was president, Buchanan visited Wheatland occasionally, but never for very long. When his term was over, he retired to his beloved mansion in 1861. He died in a room on the second floor on June 1, 1868. After a succession of owners, Wheatland, along with 5 acres of land was purchased by the James Buchanan Foundation for the Preservation of Wheatland in 1935. It was designated a National Historic Landmark in 1961 and was listed on the National Registrar of Historic Places in 1966.

The house is complimented by exquisite gardens, a carriage house, ice house, frog pond and privy. You may feel, as I did, that a visit to Wheatland celebrates a period of American history to be fondly recalled and often revisited.

Return to your car and turn left back onto PA-23 W. Head northwest for approximately 12 miles. When you get to PA-441, make a left turn and head south toward the river town of Columbia. Continue into Columbia (PA-441 becomes North Third Street). Make a right turn on Locust Street and then a left on South 2nd Street. Just after I Avenue and before Cherry Street will be the **Wright's Ferry Mansion** (38 South Second Street) on your right.

Originally constructed in 1738 by Susanna Wright, the house reflects English Quaker elegance and simplicity. This two-and-a-half story early Georgian-style limestone house is distinguished by a rich combination of artistic, academic, and cultural motifs that underscore Susanna's eclectic and diverse interests. Throughout the house you will discover a superlative collection of Philadelphia furniture, English ceramics, needlework, metals, and glass, all produced prior to 1750. In 1979 the house was listed on the National Register of Historic Places.

James Buchanan's Wheatland

Wright's Ferry Mansion in Columbia

SCENIC TOUR #3—DOWN ALONG THE RIVER

Estimated length: 31 miles
Estimated time: 1–1.5 hours

This tour is one of my all-time favorites in Lancaster County. My wife and I have driven these roads many times (in different seasons) and never tire of the incredible views and picturesque scenery. You, too, will be able to see parts of Lancaster County few visitors do—but parts that will both dazzle and amaze no matter what the season.

Begin this tour in downtown Lancaster. Drive down US-222 S/PA-272 S. Look for the large green traffic sign (overhead) denoting the exit for PA-324 S. Bear right onto PA-324 S and drive for 2.8 miles. You'll quickly escape the cacophony of the big city and begin entering the quiet and solitude of rural Lancaster County. Your journey will take you through tall rows of trees on both sides

Along River Road

of the road. You'll arrive at a traffic signal (Millersville Road/Marticville Road). Make a left turn to continue on PA-324. After half a mile you'll come to another traffic signal (PA-741). Continue straight through the signal to stay on PA-324 S.

After 1.2 miles you'll come to a stop sign. Continue straight ahead on PA-324 S for 4.2 miles. Again, you'll be traveling through a tunnel of trees on both sides of the road. You'll then arrive at another stop sign. Bear right at this stop sign and you'll continue on PA-324 (the road is also known as Pequea Boulevard). After about 3 miles you'll notice Pequea Creek Recreation Center on your left side (a great place to stop for a picnic).

After a little more than 1 mile, you'll arrive at a stop sign. The mighty Susquehanna River will be directly in front of you. If you were to turn left you would discover the tiny town of Pequea just over the bridge. However, you want to make a right turn onto River Hill Road. After about 1.7 miles you'll come to a Y in the road. Bear left at the Y to remain on River Hill Road. After 1 mile you'll come to a stop sign. Make a left turn at the stop sign onto River Road.

The journey along River Road is as peaceful and quiet as you'd ever want to imagine. This is certainly one of the most beautiful sections of Lan-

> **F**AST FACT: The Susque-hanna River drains nearly half the land area of Pennsylvania.

caster County. In spots, this road twists and turns, but it never lacks for dramatic views and scenic vistas. After about 4.5 miles you'll be traveling through Conestoga River Park on your left and Safe Harbor Park on your right. When you come to the stop sign, make a left turn to continue on River Road (it's called Groff Avenue on the right). There will also be a sign with an arrow pointing left indicating that Columbia is 9 miles away.

After driving for a while, you'll come to a T intersection (Letort Road) with a stop sign. Make a left turn in order to remain on River Road. Continue on this picturesque section of the road which fronts the Susquehanna River. You'll pass by the intersection with PA-999 and continue on River Road into the historic and vibrant town of Columbia. This would be a great opportunity to view all the historical offerings of this town (see Chapter 4) or to visit one of its classic eateries. One of my favorite restaurants is **Prudhommes' Lost Cajun Kitchen** (50 Lancaster Ave.), where you can get, among other delights, authentic fried alligator tail from Louisiana.

SCENIC TOUR #4—ALONG AMISH ROADS

Estimated length: 45 miles

Estimated time: 1.5–2 hours

Begin this picturesque tour at the intersection of US-30 and PA-340 E. Head east on PA-340 for 2.5 miles. The first town you'll come to is Smoketown, which hugs both sides of PA-340 and then you'll arrive at the intersection of PA-340 and PA-896. After PA-896 you'll begin to see a profusion of signs that lets you know you're definitely in Amish country—signs for smorgasbords, buggy rides, and authentic Amish crafts.

Along the way you'll begin to see Amish farms, wide-open spaces, corn fields, and other agricultural items. Soon you'll arrive at the intersection of PA-340 and PA-772 and the famously named town of Intercourse.

From here, the vista opens up to farmland, gently rolling hills, lots of

FAST FACT: As you might expect, signs for the town of Intercourse are often stolen. However, the town with the most frequently stolen sign may well be the borough of Shitterton in Dorset, England.

cornfields and small towns. 5.9 miles after Intercourse is the town of White Horse. From White Horse, drive for 2.7 miles and make a left turn onto Churchtown Road. Notice the farmland all around you and the dynamic farms that go along with them. About 1.4 miles after turning on Churchtown Road, you'll see an Amish one-room schoolhouse on the left side.

When you come to Mount Pleasant Road, bear left to stay on Churchtown Road. Lots of Amish farms, lots of farmland, and lots of animals can be found on both sides of the road. When you come to the stop sign at Cambridge Road, bear right to continue on Churchtown Road. You'll come to a stop sign at PA-322. Make a left onto PA-322 W.

Lancaster County has nearly 6,000 farms.

Continue on PA-322 and you'll see some small towns such as Beartown and Fetterville. Keep an eye out for produce stands on both sides of the road. You'll soon arrive in the town of Blue Ball. Make a left turn at the traffic signal for PA-23. You'll travel through the much larger town of New Holland. New Holland has all the offerings of a big town along with an eclectic array of small-town shops and boutiques.

One of the distinctive features of PA-23 is the profusion of Amish horses and buggies along the route—particularly on Sundays. Shortly after New Holland, you'll come into the very charming town of Leola. Continue on PA-23. As you get closer to Lancaster, you'll notice that the houses change in terms of architecture, design, and ambiance—particularly as you approach the area around the Lancaster Country Club.

When you get to US-30, you can head east on US-30 for about 2 miles to arrive back at your starting point.

How about a round of miniature golf?

6 Family Adventures
KID-FRIENDLY ATTRACTIONS

If you're visiting Lancaster with the kids, you'll discover an incredible variety of worthwhile attractions scattered throughout the county. Children will find plenty to keep them occupied and amused; and parents will celebrate all the county offers for families. This is indeed a wonderland for everyone—young and old.

FARMS AND FARM TOURS

Barnyard Kingdom (717-872-1554; www.countrybarnmkt.com), 211 South Donerville Road, Lancaster. Visit a real working farm. The whole family can walk through a giant 5-acre corn maze, cheer for their favorite swine at regularly scheduled pig races, tour a working farm on one of the wagon rides, and visit sheep, goats, chickens, ponies, bunnies, and more at the petting zoo.

Cherry Crest Adventure Farm (717-866-546-1799; www.cherrycrestadventure farm.com), 150 Cherry Hill Road, Ronks. This place will provide every member of the family with an authentic Lancaster County farm experience. There's a corn maze, guided wagon tours, a singing chicken show, a giant hay chute slide, a barnyard jump, and more than 50 additional farm activities.

Farmland Fun at Verdant View (717-687-7353; www.farmlandfun.com), 429 Strasburg Road, Paradise Township. The Farmland Fun tour gives families a glimpse into life on a real working farm in Lancaster County. Operated by life-long dairy farmers, the educational tour is suitable for adults and children and includes interaction with the farm animals, a tour of the working dairy farm, and various optional activities including hand milking a cow, bottle feeding a calf, and a wagon ride.

Flying M Stable (717-875-2652; www.manheimdellflyingmstable.com), 400 Shreiner Road, Leola. Located next to the Conestoga River, the Flying M Stable is a family-run horse stable located on a working cattle farm. They provide riding lessons in a range of skill levels and offer horse lovers numerous opportunities to cater to their inner cowboys (and cowgirls).

Kreider Dairy Farm Tour (717-665-5039; www.kreiderfarms.com/farm tour.php), 1455 Lancaster Road (Rt. 72), Manheim. Take the family on a 90-minute tour of a working dairy farm. Narrated bus trips through a dairy barn are highlighted by lots of farm facts.

MINIATURE GOLF

Boulders Miniature Golf Course (717-285-7007; www.bouldersmini golf.com), Route 30, Mountville Exit, Mountville. Take the family for some miniature golf on a landscaped adventure course featuring 19 challenging holes. The whole family can experience the roar of cascading waterfalls while crossing over streams and ponds seven times on various footbridges winding through the boulders.

Lost Treasure Golf and Maze (717-391-8234; www.losttreasuregolf.com), 2521 Lincoln Highway East, Ronks. Join the Expedition Guides at this miniature golf course as you follow in the footsteps of Professor Ephraim "Duffer" A. Hacker's expeditions and his search for gold and diamonds. The expeditions will take you and your family through caves and volcanoes, over waterfalls, and around cliffs as you search for "lost treasure."

Village Greens Miniature Golf (717-687-6933; www.villagegreens.com), 1444 Village Road (Route 741 West), Strasburg. The Village Greens combines the challenge of golf with the natural beauty of lush gardens to create a unique recreation experience for everyone. Two courses cover more than 13 acres of beautiful countryside enhanced with shrubbery and flowers. The courses change as the season progresses: from yellow daffodils in spring, to colorful annuals in mid-summer, to vibrant foliage in the fall.

Waters Edge Mini Golf (717-768-4653; www.watersedgegolf.net), 230 North Ronks Road, Bird-in-Hand. Waters Edge is a beautifully landscaped, water filled miniature golf course located in Bird-In-Hand. This is a family destination that is both challenging and relaxing. You can test your skills amid cascading waterfalls, gently rolling streams, and serene ponds.

PRETZELS/PRETZEL FACTORIES

Intercourse Pretzel Factory (717-768-3432; www.intercoursepretzel factory.com), 3614 Old Philadelphia Pike (at Cross Keys), Intercourse. Bring the family and watch pretzels being made right in front of you. They'll also teach you how to twist one yourself on the free tour.

Julius Sturgis Pretzel Factory (717-626-4354; www.juliussturgis.com), 219 East Main Street, Lititz. This

FAST FACT: In the 17th century, pretzels were known as "marriage knots." During a wedding ceremony a couple would wish upon a pretzel, break it, and then eat it to signify their oneness.

Let's make some pretzels!

iconic bakery claims to be the "first commercial pretzel bakery in America." You can tour the original factory, watch pretzels being twisted by hand, and create your own special pretzel (which you get to keep . . . or eat).

TRAINS

Choo Choo Barn—Traintown USA (717-687-7911; www.choochoobarn .com), 226 Gap Road (Route 741 East), Strasburg. In business since 1961, the Choo Choo Barn/Traintown USA has a 1,700-square-foot train layout that features over 150 hand-built animated figures and vehicles and 22 operating trains. If the kids love trains, they will absolutely love this place!

Strasburg Rail Road (717-687-7522; www.StrasburgRailRoad.com), Route

Everybody loves riding on the Strasburg Rail Road.

741 East, Strasburg. All aboard! The Strasburg Railroad bills itself as "America's oldest short-line railroad." Climb aboard one of these classic trains and you'll be able to ride in an authentically restored passenger car pulled by a huge, coal-burning steam locomotive. You can choose from First-Class, Open Air, Coach, and more. The Strasburg Rail Road is one of Lancaster County's most popular tourist attractions and you'll understand why after just a few minutes on this "can't miss" attraction.

OTHER KID-FRIENDLY ATTRACTIONS

Dutch Wonderland (717-386-2839; www.dutchwonderland.com), 2249 Lincoln Highway East, Lancaster. As they say, "You can't miss it!" And you certainly can't miss it as you travel along Route 30 on the east side of Lancaster. With its imposing castle and enormous parking lot you know you've arrived at every child's dream. Here you'll find more than 30 rides that include everything from trains to boats and carousels to roller coasters. There are story times, staged shows, and an all-inclusive water park. This place is Disneyland in miniature—a place the whole family can enjoy in one very active day.

Hands-on-House, Children's Museum of Lancaster (717-569-5437; www.handsonhouse.org), 721 Landis Valley Road, Lancaster. Geared for children aged 2 to 10, this interactive museum features self-directed exhibits that are designed for adults and children to play and learn together. This place is packed with indoor and outdoor activities perfect for young families.

Lancaster Science Factory (717-509-6363; www.lancastersciencefactory.org), 454 New Holland Ave., Lancaster. The Lancaster Science Factory is a hands-on, interactive technology

Dutch Wonderland

Turkey Hill Experience in Columbia

and science center. Kids will enjoy exploring the exciting exhibits on the physical sciences, engineering, technology, and mathematics.

High Sports (717-626-8318; www .highsports.com), 727 Furnace Hills Pike, Lititz. There's something for everyone in the family at this all-inclusive sports emporium. A 20-hole miniature golf course, a driving range, batting cages, baseball and slow-pitch softball, a go-cart track, and a snack bar will keep everyone happy for many hours.

Refreshing Canopy Zip Lines (717-738-1490; www.refreshingmountain .com), 455 Camp Road, Stevens. Here's a family adventure you don't see everyday. Get harnessed into a pulley and zip from platform to platform through a canopy of trees. There are two courses to choose from, both providing a refreshing aspect of the forest and wildlife.

Turkey Hill Experience (1-888-986-8784; www.turkeyhillexperience.com), 301 Linden Street, Columbia. Come learn how ice cream is made, sit in an authentic milk truck, brainstorm your own ice cream flavor, milk a mechanical cow, and learn all about the dairy industry in Lancaster County. Of course, there are free samples of Turkey Hill ice cream.

Wolf Sanctuary of PA (717-626-4617; www.wolfsancpa.org), 465 Speedwell Forge Road, Lititz. This is a family adventure well worth the trip. Quietly secluded on 20 acres of natural woodland, you will find the home of the Speedwell Wolves. For more than 30 years this site has offered refuge to wolves who have found themselves without a place in the natural world. Visit these unique creatures and help support this incredible sanctuary.

The Susquehanna River offers lots of recreational opportunities.

7 Recreation
FOR THE FUN OF IT

If you want to recreate, Lancaster County has what you're looking for! Here you can immerse yourself in an enormous variety of recreational activities guaranteed to get the adrenaline pumping, the senses stimulated, and the blood rushing. Indulge in one or more of these activities and make your visit to Lancaster complete.

BASEBALL

Lancaster Barnstormers Baseball (717-509-HITS; www.lancasterbarnstormers .com), Clipper Magazine Stadium, 650 North Prince Street, Lancaster. See some of the finest minor league baseball around in this impressive stadium. The games are exciting and the prices for tickets and food won't require a second mortgage on your home.

BOWLING

Blue Ball Lanes (717-354-5555; www.blueballlanes.com), 1214 Main St., Blue Ball. Here's an all-inclusive bowling alley with youth programs, parties, tournaments, and leagues—lots to do for every member of the family.

Leisure Bowling and Golfing Center (717-392-2121; www.leisurelanespa.com), 3440 Columbia Avenue, Lancaster. It's all here: 52 bowling lanes, a lighted golf driving range, a real-grass 18-hole putting course, an 18-hole miniature golf course, billiard room, game room, and snack bar.

GOLF COURSES

Four Seasons Golf Course (717-898-0104; www.4seasonsgolfcourse.com), 949 Church Street, Landisville. The Four Seasons has been in operation for over 50

Clipper Stadium, where the Lancaster Barnstormers play

years. This exquisitely landscaped par-70 gold course is perfect for any player, no matter what your handicap.

Lancaster Host Golf Resort (717-397-7756; www.lancasterhost.com), 2300 Lincoln Highway East, Lancaster. Recognized by Golf Digest as one of the top 100 Golf Courses in Pennsylvania, this par-71 course features 6,849 yards of golf from the longest tees. Water comes into play on seven holes, and the course rating is 70.8. Legends of the game such as Arnold Palmer, Sam Snead, and Jack Nicklaus have played here.

Willow Valley Golf Course (717-464-4448; www.WillowValley-Golf.com), 2400 Willow Street Pike, Lancaster. For only $24, you can ride the nine holes of this course or walk it for $15. The course is always in great condition and there have been several changes done over the years to create a more challenging setup and fast green speeds. There are substantial discounts for seniors (50+).

THEATERS/STAGE

American Music Theatre (1-800-648-4102; www.AMTshows.com), 2425 Lincoln Highway East (Route 30), Lancaster. For some of the best live music anywhere around, you can't beat AMT. Everything from rock to jazz to classical to hip hop to reggae to "oldies but goodies" can be found here. International and national music stars are a staple of this delightful venue.

Lancaster Host Golf Resort

American Music Theater

Bird-in-Hand Stage at the Bird-in-Hand Family Restaurant (800-790-4069; www.Bird-in-Hand.com), 2760 Old Philadelphia Pike (Route 340), Bird-in-Hand. Theater with an Amish slant is on the bill here. Original plays and dynamic musicals geared for the whole family offer some unique perspectives on Amish life and customs.

Dutch Apple Dinner Theatre (717-898-1900; www.DutchApple.com), 510 Centreville Road, Lancaster. As soon as you enter this 384-seat theater, you'll be seated at a table and invited to graze the dinner buffet. After the meal, you'll sit back and enjoy a musical featuring up-and-coming stars. Recent presentations include South Pacific, Cats, Mary Poppins, A Christmas Carol, Menopause the Musical, and How to Succeed in Business Without Really Trying.

Fulton Theatre (717-397-7425; www.thefulton.org), 12 North Princess Street, Lancaster. Central Pennsylvania's premier regional theatre and National Historic Landmark combines Broadway-caliber musicals, comedies, and dramas with the grandeur of Victorian architecture. Recent productions include Gypsy, Singing in the Rain, A Chorus Line, Witness for the Prosecution, Dreamgirls, Joseph and the Amazing Technicolor Dreamcoat, and Anne of Green Gables.

Lancaster County Comedy Show (717-687-4263; www.lancastercountycomedy show.com), 202 Hartman Bridge Road, Ronks. Lancaster County Comedy Show is a theatrically produced ventriloquist show full of comedy and songs for all ages. Ventriloquist Ryan is joined by little Jakey, the Amish boy, Harold & Irene, retired farmers, Tiffany the tourist, and Ardie the Skunk as they explore Lancaster County with some hilarious results.

The Fulton—a classic theater

Sight and Sound Theaters

Lancaster Symphony Orchestra (717-291-6440; www.lancastersymphony.org), 226 North Arch Street, Lancaster. The Lancaster Symphony Orchestra has hosted dozens of internationally renowned artists and presented countless U.S. and world premieres, all while maintaining a world-class professional orchestra.

Rainbow Dinner Theatre (800-292-4301; www.rainbowdinnertheatre.com), 3065 Lincoln Highway east, Paradise. The Rainbow Dinner Theatre is an all-comedy dinner theatre. It's a place for the whole family to enjoy some fine dining and lots of laughs.

Sight and Sound Theatres (1-800-377-1277; www.sight-sound.com), 300 Hartman Bridge Road, Strasburg. The multi-layered plays and extravagant musicals here are all Christian-based and revolve around common biblical stories, parables, or figures. Each production is geared for all members of the family.

VINEYARDS, WINERIES, AND BREWERIES

Brandywine Valley Wine Trail (610-444-3842; www.bvwinetrail.com), 5697 Strasburg Road, Gap, PA 17527. The Brandywine Valley Wine Trail offers a unique assortment of festivals, celebrations, and tours throughout the region.

Bube's Brewery (717-653-2056; www.bubesbrewery.com), 102 North Market Street, Mount Joy. Bube's Brewery is an intact historic 19th-century brewery, restaurant, and museum complex.

Lancaster Brewing Company (717-391-6258; www.lancasterbrewing.com), 302 North Plum Street, Lancaster. The Lancaster Brewing Company handcrafts its own ales and lagers and has an extensive lunch and dinner menu.

Iron Hill Brewery and Restaurant (717-291-9800; www.ironhillbrewery.com), 781 Harrisburg Pike, Lancaster. At the Iron Hill Brewery & Restaurant you'll find fine handcrafted beers, creative yet informal cuisine, and an eclectic menu in a casual, upscale atmosphere.

Nissley Vineyards and Winery Estate (717-426-3514; www.nissleywine.com), 140 Vintage Drive, Bainbridge. Nissley is a family-owned and -operated winery

A Lancaster County vineyard

(for 35 years) in Lancaster County. Here you can sample their many varieties of white and red wines.

Rumspringa Brewing Company (717-768-7194; www.lancaster-gallery.com), 3174 Old Philadelphia Pike, Bird-in-Hand. Located on the second floor of the Lancaster Beer & Wine Gallery, this is the area's first nano-brewery, which produces tastes as varied as a citrus-y IPA to a robust Stout.

Stoudt's Brewery and Beer Festivals (717-484-4386; www.stoudts.com), 2800 North Reading Road (Route 272 North), Adamstown. Stoudt's Brewing Company is an ideal destination for beer lovers. As one of the pioneering craft breweries, Stoudt's offers a variety of lagers and ales.

Strasburg Winery (717-288-2385; www.strasburg.com), 11 West Main Street, Strasburg. Featuring an extensive list of seasonal and classic wines, the winery offers free wine tasting and wines by the bottle and glass. They also have a wide selection of wine-related gifts, from handcrafted glasses to iron cork cages.

Thorn Hill Vineyards California Tasting Room (717-517-7839; www.thornhill vineyards.com), 1945 Fruitville Pike, Lancaster. Thorn Hill Vineyards focuses on

The Strasburg Winery

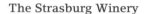

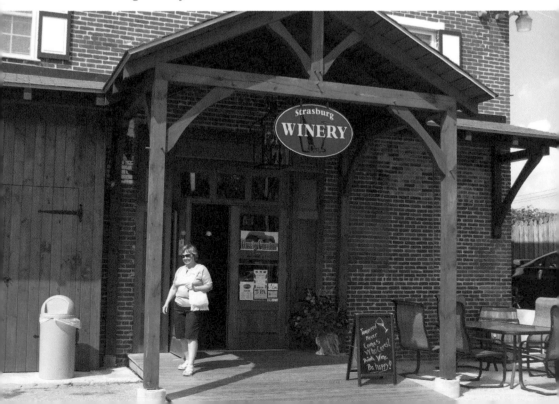

limited production of red Bordeaux varietals and small lots of Chardonnay, and Petite Sirah.

Twin Brook Winery (717-442-4915; www.twinbrookwinery.com), 5697 Strasburg Road, Gap. Twin Brook offers a selection of award-winning wines, spectacular entertainment, and a stunning Lancaster County landscape.

Vineyard at Grandview (717-653-4825; www.thevineyardatgrandview.com), 1489 Grandview Road, Mount Joy. This is a family-owned vineyard in the rolling hills of northern Lancaster County specializing in Cabernet Sauvignon, Merlot and Chardonnay.

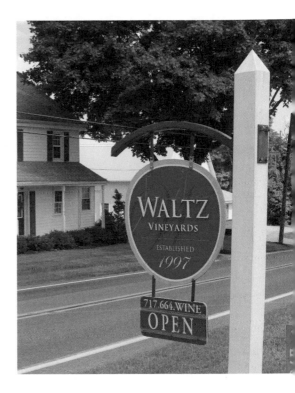

Waltz Vineyards & Winery (717-664-WINE; www.waltzvineyards.com), 1599 Old Line Road, Manheim. Situated on a beautiful hill between Lancaster and Lebanon, this sixth-generation family farm boasts a unique micro-climate and world-class vineyard soils.

WATER ACTIVITIES

Mount Gretna Lake & Beach (717-964-3130; www.mtgretnalake.com), 130 Lakeview Drive, Lebanon. Spend a day at the lake with tons of water activities for the whole family. Swimming areas, a sandy beach, picnic tables, a snack bar, over-water swings, tube rentals, diving boards, kayak rentals, volleyball court, play areas, and lots of free parking make for a perfect summer day.

Susquehanna River Water Trail (717-252-0229; www.susquehannawatertrail.org). This section of the Susquehanna is a 53-mile-long paddler's adventure that begins at the New Market Boat Access near Harrisburg and ends a few miles south of the Mason-Dixon Line in Maryland. It offers a tremendous diversity of natural and built environments. Check out the website for all the maps and guides.

Candy & ice cream—two of life's greatest pleasures!

8 Shopping
STORES YOU WON'T BELIEVE!

From A (antiques) to Z (zebra-skin rugs), it's all here in Lancaster County. Whether you're on the main roads (US-30, PA-340) or along a country road that stretches out toward the horizon, you're sure to find a dynamic assembly of stores, shops, markets and other shopping venues—both large and small that will entice you with unique wares and equally unique values. There are many treasures to be found throughout Lancaster County, so warm up your checkbook and rev up your credit cards—you're in for many a delightful discovery.

ANTIQUES

If you come to Lancaster County and don't take advantage of all the incredible antique retailers in the area, then you will have truly missed a most unique experience! If you are an aficionado of old stuff, then this is your place. The variety of offerings will amaze you and there are bargains to be had around every corner.

Lancaster County has an abundance of antiques shops.

Antiques Capital U.S.A. (www.antiquescapital.com), Adamstown.

Bird-in-Hand Old Village Store and Antique Market (717-397-1291; www .oldvillagestore.vpweb.com), 2705 Old Philadelphia Pike, Bird-in-Hand.

The Black Horse Antiques Mall & Showcase (717-336-8447; www.black horselodge.com), 2152 North Reading Road, Denver.

Building Character (717-394-7201; www.buildingcharacter.biz), 342 North Queen Street, Warehouse B, Lancaster.

Burning Bridge Antiques Market (717-684-7900; www.burningbridgeantiques .com), 304 Walnut Street, Columbia.

Cackleberry Farm Antique Mall (717-442-8805; www.cackleberryfarmantique mall.com), 3371 Lincoln Highway East (Route 30), Paradise.

Don & Ann's Antique Roe (717-517-2014), 2705 Old Philadelphia Pike, Bird-in-Hand.

Renninger's Antique and Collectables Market (717-336-2177; www
.renningers.com), Route 272, Adamstown.

Stoudt's Black Angus Antiques
Mall (717-484-2757; www.stoudts
.com), 2800 North Reading Road
(route 272 North), Adamstown.

White Horse Mill Antique and Art
Gallery (717-768-0960; www.white
horsemill.com), 101 West Cambridge
Road, Gap.

BAKERIES

The aroma of freshly baked bread
wafting in the air, the scent of homemade sticky buns greeting you as you
enter a shop, and the smell of classic
chocolate-chip cookies lets you know
that you are in, what may arguably be,
the bakery capital of the world. Please

don't return home without visiting one of Lancaster County's classic and distinctive bakeries.

Achenbach's Pastry (717-656-6671; www.achenbachs.com), 375 East Main
Street, Leola.

Bird-in-Hand Bake Shop (717-656-7947; www.bihbakeshop.com), 542 Gib-
bons Road, Bird-in-Hand.

Bird-in-Hand Bakery and Creamery (1-800-524-3429; www.bird-in-hand.
com), 2715 Old Philadelphia Pike (Route 340), Bird-in-Hand.

Dutch Haven Shoo-Fly Pie Bakery & Gift Shop (717-687-0111; www.dutch
haven.com), 2857A Lincoln Highway East, Ronks.

Fisher's Bakery & Roadside Stand (717-768-3541), 328 North Belmont Road,
Gordonville.

Ahhh—the smell of a bakery!

La Dolce Vita Courthouse Bakery (717-239-5101; www.ladolcevitalancaster
.com), 9 North Duke Street, Lancaster.

Miller's Bakery and Gift Shop (717-687-6621; www.millars1929.com), 2811
Lincoln Highway East (Route 30), Ronks.

Mr. Sticky's Homemade Sticky Buns (717-413-9229; www.mrsticky.com), 501
Greenfield Road, Lancaster.

Ric's Breads (717-392-8385; www.ricsbreads.com), 24 North Queen Street,
Lancaster.

Willow Valley Bakery (717-464-2716; www.WillowValley-Restaurant.com),
2416 Willow Street Pike, Lancaster.

BOOKS

Besides an array of commercial big-box bookstores scattered along the highways of Lancaster County, there are several smaller mom-and-pop stores that offer a unique selection of titles, books ,and authors you will probably find nowhere else.

DogStar Books (717-823-6605; www.dogstarbooks.com), 401 West Lemon Street.

Gordonville Book Store (717-768-3512), 275 Old Leacock Road, Gordonville.

Legacy Used Books & Collectables (717-351-0740; www.legacyusedbooksand collectables.com), 145 East Main Street, New Holland.

Main Street Book Shop and Gallery (717-768-7171; www.MainStreetBooks AndGallery.com), 3518 Old Philadelphia Pike, Intercourse.

CANDLES

Homemade candles have a scent and a history that you won't find in any department stores. These treasures are crafted by folks who truly know the meaning of "homemade." Let your senses take a wild trip in these most distinctive shops.

Big Bear Candle & Gifts (717-687-9003; www.IBelieveSanta.com), 2821 Lincoln Highway East, Ronks.

The Old Candle Barn (717-768-8926; www.oldcandlebarn.com), 3551 Old Philadelphia Pike, Intercourse.

FARMERS' MARKETS

Ask the locals for the one commercial enterprise that distinguishes Lancaster County and many folks will tell you it's the farmer's markets. Here is where the pulse of the county can be felt and where you'll have an opportunity to chat with some of the most pleasant and engaging people around. Spend a morning in a farmer's market and you'll pick up much more than a bushel full of produce.

Bird-in-Hand Farmer's Market (717-393-9674; www.birdinhandfarmers market.com), 2710 Old Philadelphia Pike (Route 340), Bird-in-Hand.

Central Market (717-291-4723; www.centralmarketlancaster.com), 23 North Market Street, Lancaster.

Bird-in-Hand Farmer's Market

Cherry Hill Orchards (717-872-9311; www.cherryhillorchards.com), 400 Long Lane (Route 324 at Route 741), Lancaster.

Columbia Market (717-449-4731; www.columbiahistoricmarkethouse.com), 3rd and Locust Streets, Columbia.

Green Dragon Farmers Market and Auction (717-738-1117; www.green dragonmarket.com), 955 North State Street, Ephrata.

Kaufman's Fruit Farm and Market (717-768-7112; www.kauffmansfruitfarm .com), 3097 Old Philadelphia Pike, Bird-in-Hand.

Stoudt's Wonderful Good Market (717-484-2757; www.stoudts.com), 2800 North Reading Road (Route 272 North), Adamstown.

Village Farm Market (717-733-5340; www.villagefarmmarket.com), 1520 Division Highway (Route 322), Ephrata.

FURNITURE

Handcrafted furniture has long been a tradition in Lancaster County. Lovingly detailed chairs, exquisitely finished tables and amazingly rich bedroom pieces will command your attention and respect. This is furniture you won't find in big chain stores; this is furniture done the right way—by hand.

Country Home Furniture (717-354-2329; www.chfs1.com), At Shady Maple, 1352 Main Street, East Earl.

Fisher's Quality Furniture (717-656-4423; www.fishersqualityfurniture.com), 3061 West Newport Road, Ronks.

George's Woodcrafts (717-426-1004; www.georgeswood.com), 9 Reichs Church Road, Marietta.

Gish's Furniture—Amish Heirlooms (1-866-925-4474; www.gishs.com), 2191 Lincoln Highway East (Route 30), Lancaster.

Stoudt's Wonderful Good Market

Kauffman's Handcrafted Clocks (717-656-4354; www.KHClock.com), 3019 West Newport Road, Ronks.

Lapp's Coach Shop (717-768-8712; www.lappscoachshop.com), 3572 West Newport Road, Intercourse.

Lapp's Toys and Furniture (717-768-7243; www.lappstoysandfurniture.com), 3022 Irishtown Road, Ronks.

Martin's Chair (717-355-2177; www.martinschair.com), 124 King Court, New Holland.

Morton Fine Furniture (717-656-3799; www.mortonfurniture.com), 61 East Main Street, Lititz.

Old Road Furniture Company (717-768-0478; www.oldroadfurniture.com), 3457 Old Philadelphia Pike, Intercourse.

Peaceful Valley Amish Furniture (717-687-8336; www.peacefulvalley furniture.com), 421 Hartman Bridge Road, Strasburg.

Snyder's Furniture (717-768-7642; www.synydersfurniture.com), 3709 East Newport Road, Gordonville.

Tellus360 (717-393-1660; www.tellus360.com), 24 East King Street, Lancaster.

Wolf Rock Furniture (717-442-8990; www.wolfrockfurniture.com), 3533 Lincoln Highway East, Kinzers.

GLASS

If you've never seen glass produced—especially by skilled artisans—then you'll definitely want to take the family to one of the shops below. This is an adventure for the eyes of both young and old alike.

Art & Glassworks (717-394-4133; www.artandglassworks.com), 319 North Queen Street, Lancaster.

Susquehanna Glass (717-684-2155, Ext. 109; www.theglassfactory.com), 731 Avenue H, Columbia.

MEATS AND CHEESES

Do you want to treat your taste buds to something they've never experienced before? Then set your course to one of these shops and sample some of the best aged cheeses and delightful meats you'll never find in your local supermarket at home. Load up on these goodies and take them home. Your friends will be incredibly jealous.

S. Clyde Weaver—Smoked Meats & Cheese (717-569-0812; www.SClydeWeaver.com), 5253 Main St., East Petersburg.

Community of Oasis at Bird-in-Hand (717-288-2154; www.reallivefood.org), 60 North Ronks Road, Ronks.

Groffdale Meadows Cheese (717-656-2946; www.groffdalemeadows.com), 225 Voganville Road., New Holland.

September Farm Cheese (610-273-3552; www.septemberfarmcheese.com), 460 Mill Road., Honey Brook.

The Smokehouse Shop (717-768-3805; www.thesmokehouseshop.com), Kitchen Kettle Village, 3529 Old Philadelphia Pike, Intercourse.

Stoltzfus Meats & Deli (717-768-7287; www.stoltzfusmeats.com), 14 Center Street, Intercourse.

ONE-OF-A-KIND STORES

There is no way to describe the stores and shops in this section, other than to say that you won't find anything similar in your hometown. And that's the beauty of these places—they are singular, they are unique, and they are definitely one-of-a-kind. Check them out!

Authentic Lancaster (717-940-2655; www.AuthenticLancaster.com), 3545 Marietta Pike, Building S, Lancaster.

The BeadWorks and Gem Den (717-490-6551; www.thegemgarden.com), 52 North Queen Street, Lancaster.

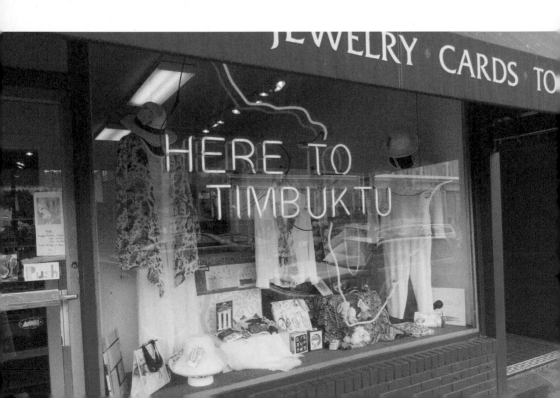

Building Character (717-394-7201; www.buildingcharacter.biz), rear warehouses at 342 North Queen Street, Lancaster.

Burkholder Fabrics (717-336-6692; www.burkfabrics.com), 2155 West Route 897, Denver.

Choo Choo Barn (717-687-7911; www.choochoobarn.com), Route 741 East, Strasburg.

The Deerskin Leather Shop (1-800-732-3538, Ext. 327; www.kitchenkettle.com/deerskin.html), At Kitchen Kettle Village, 3529 Old Philadelphia Pike, Intercourse.

Eastland Alpacas (717-653-2757; www.eastlandalpacas.com), 2089 Risser Mill Road, Mount Joy.

Fisher's Housewares & Fabrics (717-786-8121), 1098 Georgetown Road, Bart.

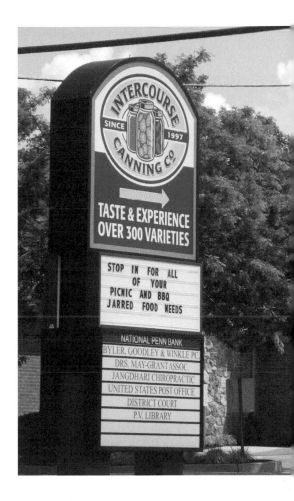

Fresco Green Scene (717-517-8715; www.frescogreen.com), 104 West Chestnut Street, Lancaster.

Gem Garden (717-664-5522; www.gemgardenjewelers.com), 1575 Lebanon Road (Route 72), Manheim.

The Good Cooking Store (717-768-3032; www.TheGoodCookingStore.com), 3474 Old Philadelphia Pike (Route 340), Intercourse.

Good Food Outlet Store (717-656-3486; www.goldenbarrel.com), 388 East Main Street (Route 23), Leola.

Here to Timbuktu (717-293-8595; www.heretotimbuktu.com), 46 North Prince Street, Lancaster.

Intercourse Canning Company (717-768-0156; www.intercoursecanning.com), 3612 East Newport Road (Route 772), Intercourse.

Jam & Relish Kitchen (1-800-732-3538; www.kitchenkettle.com), At Kitchen Kettle Village, 3529 Old Philadelphia Pike, Intercourse.

Kitchen Kettle Village (800-732-3538; www.kitchenkettle.com), 3529 Old Philadelphia Pike, Intercourse. Mon.-Sat., 9 AM-6 PM (November to April until 5 PM).

Lancaster Bead Company (717-823-6817), 2481 Lincoln Highway East, Lancaster.

Mommalicious (717-299-0827; www.mommalicious.com), 310 North Queen Street, Lancaster.

Olio Olive Oils and Balsamics (717-627-0088; www.OlioOliveOil.com), 41B South Broad Street, Lititz.

Rohrer Seeds (717-299-2571; www.rohrerseeds.com), 2472 Old Philadelphia Pike, Smoketown.

Sam's Steins & Collectables (717-394-6404; www.samssteins.com), 2207 Lincoln Highway East, Lancaster.

Seasons Olive Oil & Vinegar Taproom (717-396-1380; www.seasonstaproom .com), 36 West King Street, Lancaster.

Smucker's Gourds (717-354-6118), 317 Springville Road, Kinzers.

Strasburg Country Store & Creamery (717-687-0766; www.strasburg.com), 1 West Main Street, Strasburg.

Strasburg Train Shop (717-687-0464; www.etrainshop.com), 226 Gap Road (Route 741 East), Strasburg.

Stoudtburg Village and Shops (www.stoudtburgvillage.com), 2800 North Reading Road (Route 272 North), Adamstown.

Susquehanna Glass Factory Outlet and Tour (717-684-2155; www.theglass factory.com), 731 Avenue H, Columbia.

Village of Dutch Delights (717-687-8826; www.outhousepa.com), 2847 Lincoln Highway East, Ronks.

Whiff Roasters Coffee (717-627-5282; www.whiffroasters.com), 219 East Main Street (Rear), Lititz.

Zanzibar Romancing Your Senses (717-390-2868; www.zanzibarshop.com), 21 West King Street, Lancaster.

Zook's Fabric Store (717-768-8153; www.zandsfabrics.com), 3535 Old Philadelphia Pike, Intercourse.

OUTLETS

Say Lancaster County and most people will instantly think of all the outlet stores
that could easily consume most of the time you're here. Visits these outlets and
you'll discover everything from shoes to kitchen ware and from toys to tuxedos
… all at substantial and significant savings. If you're looking for bargains, you
will find them here!

Rockvale Outlets (717-293-9595; www.rockvaleoutletslancaster.com), 35 South
Willowdale Drive (Routes 30 and 896), Lancaster.

Tanger Outlet Center (717-392-7260; www.tangeroutlet.com), 311 Stanley K
Tanger Boulevard N (Route 30 East), Lancaster.

POTTERY

Handmade and handcrafted pottery is a treasure for any home. Lancaster County
has some of the finest potters you'll find anywhere in the county—folks who have
been practicing their art for decades. Stop and visit these delightful shops.

Eldreth Pottery (717-687-8445; www.eldrethpottery.com), 246 North Decatur Street (on Route 896), Strasburg.

Kevin Lehman's Pottery (717-509-7547; www.klpottery.com), 560 South Prince Street, Lancaster.

Pots by de Perrot (717-627-6789; www.potsbydeperrot.com), 201 South Locust Street (Rear), Lititz.

The PotteryWorks (717-299-9963; www.thepotteryworks.com), 16 West Orange Street, Lancaster.

Village Pottery and Jewelry (717-768-7171; www.TheVillagePottery.com), 3518 Old Philadelphia Pike, Intercourse.

PRETZELS

Pretzels are one of the staples of Lancaster County. And there's a good reason why—after all, who doesn't love a good homemade pretzel? If you want some of the best made anywhere in the country, check out these places. I dare you to return home without a couple of bags of pretzels in the back seat of your car.

Keystone Pretzel Bakery & Outlet (717-560-1882; www.keystonepretzels .com), Flyway Business Park, 124 West Airport Road, Lititz.

Hammond Pretzel Bakery (717-392-7532; www.hammondpretzels.com), 716 South West End Avenue, Lancaster.

Intercourse Pretzel Factory (717-768-3432), 3614 Old Philadelphia Pike (at Cross Keys), Intercourse.

Julius Sturgis Pretzel Bakery (717-626-4354; juliussturgis.com), 219 East Main Street, Lititz.

QUILTS

Here is perhaps the quilt capital of the country. Plan a stop in just one of these stores and you'll have an opportunity to see all the love and passion that goes into a single quilt. Whether you put a Lancaster County quilt on your bed or hang it on the wall, you will know that you have found a treasure to be passed down through many generations.

BittyKinna's Quilt Shop (717-768-8885; www.bittykinna.com), 3466 Old Philadelphia Pike, Intercourse.

Good friends are like Quilts.
They age with you, yet never lose their warmth.

Country Lane Quilts (717-656-8476), 221 South Groffdale Road, Leola.

Dutchland Quilt Patch Intercourse (1-800-411-3221; www.dutchlandquilts .com), 3453 Old Philadelphia Pike (Route 340), Intercourse.

Esh's Handmade Quilts (717768-8435), 3829 Old Philadelphia Pike, Gordon-ville.

Family Farm Quilts of Intercourse (717-768-8375; www.familyfarmquilts .com), 3511 West Newport Road, Ronks.

Family Farm Quilts of Shady Maple (717-354-1772; www.quiltsofshadymaple .com), 133 Toddy Drive, East Earl.

Hannah's Quilts (717-392-4524), 216 Witmer Road, Lancaster.

J & B Quilts, 157 North Star Road, Ronks.

Lapp's Quilts and Craft Shop (717-687-8889), 206 North Star Road, Ronks.

Log Cabin Quilt Shop and Fabrics (717-393-1702; www.lcquiltshop.com), 2679 Old Philadelphia Pike, Lancaster.

The Old Country Store (717-768-7601; www.theOldCountryStore.com), 3510 Old Philadelphia Pike, Intercourse.

Piece by Piece Quilt Shop (717-738-6983; www.piecebypiecequiltshop.com), 22 North State Street, Ephrata.

The Quilt Ledger (610-593-7300; www.thequiltledger.com), 326 North Bridge Street, Christiana.

Quilt Shop at Miller's Smorgasbord (717-687-8439; www.QuiltShopAt Millers.com), 2811 Lincoln Highway East (Route 30), Ronks.

Riehl's Quilts & Crafts (717-656-0697; www.riehlsamishquilts.com), 247 East Eby Road, Leola.

Sylvia Petersheim's Quilts, Fabrics & Crafts (717-392-6404; www.sylvias quilts.com), 2544 Old Philadelphia Pike, Bird-in-Hand.

Log Cabin Quilt Shop and Fabrics

Village Quilts (717-768-2787; www.kitchenkettle.com/quilts), At Kitchen Kettle Village, 3529 Old Philadelphia Pike, Intercourse.

Witmer's Quilt Shop (717-656-9526), 1076 West Main Street (Route 23), New Holland.

SWEETS

Here's a challenge for you—just try to walk into one of these stores or shops and leave without a large bag of goodies for all your friends and family back home (assuming said treats won't be consumed in advance). Trust me—you'll definitely want to reward yourself with some of these sweets.

The Good Scoop (717-768-3032; www.GoodScoop.com), 3470 Old Philadelphia Pike, Intercourse.

The Wilbur Chocolate Company

Miesse Candies and Factory Tour (717-392-6011; www.miessecandies.com), 735 Lafayette Street, Lancaster.

Pepper Lane Fudge & Sweets (717-768-3740; www.pepperlanefudge.com), Kitchen Kettle Village (Route 340), Intercourse.

Splits & Giggles (717-399-3332; www.splitsandgigglesicecream.com), 500 West Lemon Street, Lancaster.

Wilbur Chocolate Factory Store & Candy Americana Museum (717-626-3249; www.wilburbuds.com), 48 North Broad Street, Lititz.

Olde Heritage Rootbeer (717-768-8875), 3217 Old Philadelphia Pike, Ronks.

The Springerle House Cookie & Tea Café (717-687-8022; www.springlerlehouse.com), 11 East Main Street, Strasburg.

Uncle Leroy's Ice Cream & Candy Kitchen (717-288-2557; www.uncleleroys.com), 226 Gap Road, Strasburg.

> **F**AST FACT: The average American consumes 23.2 quarts of ice cream or ice cream products every year.

YoFro Sweets Frozen Yogurt (717-399-0219), 2405 Covered Bridge Drive, Lancaster.

TOYS

Forget about all those extra-large toy stores back home. If you're looking for some distinctive one-of-a-kind toys for your kids or relatives, take a stroll through some of these shops. You'll discover some absolutely marvelous treasures.

BellaBoo (717-509-5700; www.BellaBooOnline.com), 32 North Queen Street, Lancaster.

Doll Outlet (717-687-8118; www.dolloutlet.com), 2682 Lincoln Highway East (Route 30), Ronks.

Outback Toys—Binkley & Hurst (717-625-2020; www.outbacktoystore.com), 101 West Lincoln Avenue, Lititz.

Strasburg Toys & Collectables (717-687-9288; www.strasburgtoys.com), 350 Hartman Bridge Road (Route 896), Ronks.

Saron (Sister's house) at Ephrata Cloister

9 Culture
HISTORIC SITES, MUSEUMS & THE ARTS

Whether it's a journey into the historical archives of Lancaster County, a visit to a unique museum, a cutting-edge dance ensemble, or a walk around a centuries-old homestead that faithfully captures the "good old days," you'll find it all here in Lancaster County. Culture is definitely alive—including riches both ancient and new, visual treats, and intellectual treasures that will amaze and delight. You'll leave with a deep appreciation for the incredible depth and breadth of culture that is so much a part of this vibrant region.

HISTORIC SITES AND ORGANIZATIONS

1852 Herr Family Homestead (717-898-8822; www.herrhomestead.org), 1756 Nissley Road, Landisville. This is an authentic 19th-century farm that depicts life in the earliest years of Lancaster County history. Walk through the house and along garden paths that create a true "step back in time" feeling.

Conestoga Area Historical Society (717-872-1699; http://pennmanorhistory .org), 51 Kendig Road (Ehrlich Park), Conestoga. There are seven major buildings on this museum's grounds. These include the Tobacco Shed, the Steven Atkinson log cabin, the Michael Harnish Stone House, the Elmer Hoak Broom Shop (a toll booth), the Myers Tannery Shed, a replica of a Sweitzer Bank Barn, and the Tobias Stehman Blacksmith Shop.

> **FAST FACT:** The town of Conestoga was named for the Conestoga Indians. The Conestoga wagon, used in the 18th and 19th centuries to transport cargo over the Appalachian Mountains, was named after this small town.

Visitors Center at Ephrata Cloister

Ephrata Cloister (717-733-6600; www.ephratacloister.org), 632 West Main Street, Ephrata. One of America's earliest religious communities, the Ephrata Cloister was founded in 1732 by German settlers. The museum and grounds are a step back into a time long since past. This is a must-see site for any Lancaster County visitor.

Hans Herr House and Museum (717-464-4438; www.hansherr.org), 1849 Hans Herr Drive, Willow Street. The Hans Herr House is the oldest homestead in Lancaster County. Built in 1719, it is the oldest original Mennonite meetinghouse still standing in the Western Hemisphere.

Historic Schaefferstown (717-949-2244; www.hsimuseum.org), 106 North Market Street, Schaefferstown. The Alexander Schaeffer Farm House has been designated a National Historic Landmark. The Schaeffer House is one of only 167 sites in Pennsylvania, and 2,500 nationwide, to be awarded this designation.

Mascot Roller Mills and Ressler Family Home (717-656-7616; www .resslermill.com), 443 West Newport Road, Ronks. This site features a re-markably preserved water-powered grain mill, as well as an opportunity to

> **F**AST FACT: Robert Fulton designed the first working submarine—*the Nautilus*—between 1793 and 1797.

learn about 19th-century milling techniques and procedures. The adjacent 1855 miller's house is a window into early 20th-entury housekeeping and family life.

Robert Fulton Birthplace (717-548-2594), Route 222, Robert Fulton Highway, P.O. Box 33, Quarryville. You'll be able to see what life was like in the mid-1700s as authentic reproduction furnishings have been returned to this rustic dwelling. The home looks much the way it did when Fulton was child. The simplicity of

Hans Herr House and Museum

Mascot Roller Mills and Ressler Family Home

the furnishings is a testament to the austerity of life in 18th-century Lancaster County.

Wright's Ferry Mansion (717-684-4325), Second and Cherry Streets, Columbia. This mansion has been faithfully restored and furnished with authentic trappings of the early 18th century. The furnishings are Queen Anne and Philadelphia William and Mary—a delicious blending of American and English styles. If you love antiques, then this is your place.

MUSEUMS

American Military Edged Weaponry Museum (717-768-7185), 3562 Old Philadelphia Pike, Intercourse. This is one of the country's most comprehensive collections of U.S. military knives and artifacts used by American servicemen. The knives range from pikes, swords, sabers, fencing bayonets, bowie, knuckle and trench knives. Also on display is a rocket, grease gun, flaregun, BAR & Thompson machine gun.

Christiana Underground Railroad Museum (610-593-5340; www.zerchershotel .com), 11 Green Street, Christiana. Zercher's Hotel may appear unassuming from the outside, but its place in history is anything but. For many, the events that happened here were one of the significant catalysts that sparked the Civil War. For Civil War buffs, it is well worth a visit.

Columbia Historic Preservation Society (717-684-2894; www.columbiahistory .net), 21 North 2nd Street, Columbia. In addition to offering published articles and books on Columbia's history, the museum houses a model train display, artifacts, a research room, microfilm archive, and numerous historical publications.

Landis Valley Village & Farm Museum (717-569-0401; www.landisvalley museum.org), 2451 Kissel Hill Road, Lancaster. The village and museum offer visitors a slice out of history—it's a living history village and farm that collects,

Robert Fulton Birthplace

preserves and interprets the history and material culture of the Pennsylvania German rural community from 1740 to 1940. This is a terrific family experience you won't find anywhere else.

Lititz Historical Foundation (717-627-4636; www.lititzhistoricalfoundation .com), 137-145 East Main Street, Lititz. Beautiful gardens and a 45-minute tour through the Lititz Museum Johannes Mueller House by costumed guides provide a wonderful entree into early life in this classic American small town.

Manheim Historical Society (717-665-7989; www.manheimpa.com), 88 South Grant Street, Manheim. The Manheim Historical Society owns four properties in Manheim Borough which include the Manheim Railroad Station, Manheim Heritage Center, the Fasig and Keath Houses and also the Town Clock in the Mini Park.

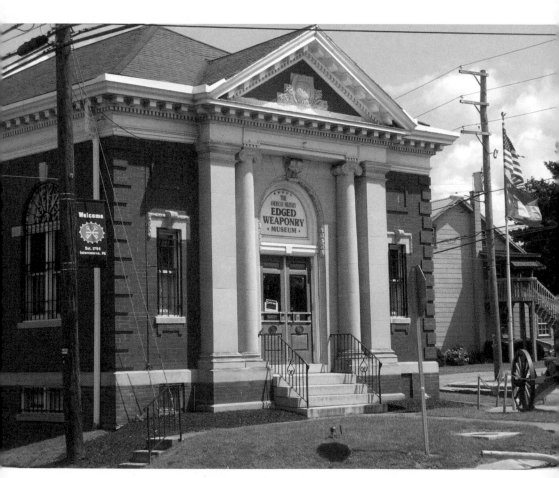

American Military Edges Weaponry Museum

The Tin Shop at Landis Valley Village

National Toy Train Museum (717-687-8976; www.nttmuseum.org), 300 Paradise Lane, Strasburg. Designed like an old-time train station, the museum features the latest in exhibits and LED lighting. The massive toy train collection features models from the 1800s to the present. Five operating, interactive train layouts in G, Standard, O, S, and HO Gauges are also displayed.

National Watch & Clock Museum (717-684-8261; www.museumoftime .org), 514 Poplar Street, Columbia. This is truly one of the most fascinating museums you'll ever see. Everything to do with time, including timepieces, the history of time, how

The Museum Store at Landis Valley Village & Farm Museum

time was discovered, how time was used, and some of the mistakes we've made in gauging time are all on display. I've been here several times and keep coming back—it's that good!

Quilt Museum at the Old Country Store (1-800-828-8218; www.ocsquilt museum.com), 3510 Old Philadelphia Pike, Intercourse. If you want to see some of the finest examples of quilts to be found anywhere in the country, then this is the place. Shows, exhibits, lectures by visiting quilters, special workshops and everything else connected with quilts is on display here.

> **F**AST FACT: Up until the late 19th century, the United States did not have time zones. Each town or region kept its own time.

Railroad Museum of Pennsylvania (717-687-8628; www.rrmuseumpa .com), 300 Gap Road (Route 741 East), Strasburg. For railroads buffs of any age this is "the Magic Kingdom." More than 100 historic locomotives and railroad cars are housed in this gigantic museum—a paean to times gone by! There are lots of hands-on activities for the kids and loads of exhibits for the adults. Put on your railroad hat (available in the well-stocked gift shop) and enjoy the journey. All aboard!

PERFORMING ARTS: THEATER

Theater is alive and well in Lancaster County. Plays by local playwrights just getting their start, Shakespearean tragedies put on by regional repertory companies, and major Broadway productions performed by national touring groups are all part of the theatrical scene in Lancaster. Pair up a theatrical performance with one of Lancaster's cutting-edge restaurants and you'll definitely have an evening to remember.

Bethel Harambee "Living the Experience" (717-509-1177), 512 East Strawberry Street, Lancaster.

Fulton Theatre (717-397-7425), 12 North Prince Street, Lancaster.

Hole in the Wall Puppet Theatre and Museum (717-394-8398), 126 North Water Street, Lancaster.

Prima Theatre Company (717-327-5124), 42 North Prince Street, Lancaster.

The People's Shakespeare Project (717-399-9385), 305 North West End Avenue, Lancaster.

National Toy Train Museum

Railroad Museum of Pennsylvania

Theater of the Seventh Sister, Stahr Performing Arts Center (717- 396-7764), 438 North Queen Street, Lancaster

Theatre for Transformation (717-333-9563), 209 Pearl Street, Lancaster.

PERFORMING ARTS: MUSIC

If you like music, then you'll definitely like what Lancaster County has to offer. Everything from classical to hip hop and opera to hard rock can be found in the clubs, cabarets, festivals, celebrations, fairs, and special performances that are so much a part of Lancaster's musical heritage.

Allegro: the Chamber Orchestra of Lancaster (717-560-7317), Barshinger Center, Franklin & Marshall College, Lancaster.

Chameleon Club (717-299-9684), 223 North Water Street, Lancaster.

Lancaster Classical Guitar Institute & Festival (717-871-7806), 42 North Prince Street, Studio 3-03, Lancaster.

Lancaster Symphony Orchestra (717-291-6440), 226 North Arch Street, Lancaster.

Long's Park Art & Craft Festival (717-735-8885), 1441 Harrisburg Pike, Lancaster.

Music at Trinity (717-397-2734), Holy Trinity Lutheran Church, 31 South Duke Street, Lancaster.

OperaLancaster (717-871-7814), 42 North Prince Street, Suite M-05, Lancaster.

PERFORMING ARTS: DANCE

Whether you're in the mood to trip the light fantastic with your partner or watch a nationally acclaimed dance troupe perform magic on the stage, you'll find everything you could hope for in Lancaster County's dance scene. You may even feel inclined to spend some time perfecting your own dance routines—after all, those contestants on TV's "Dancing with the Stars" had to start somewhere!

Argentine Tango Club of Lancaster (717-475-0045), 19 East King Street, Lancaster.

Ballet Theater of Lancaster (717-672-0826), P.O. Box 4511, Lancaster.

Ballroom on the Square (717-813-6144), 355 West Chestnut Street, Lancaster.

City Ballroom (717-380-6915), 420 West Grant Street, Lancaster.

Dance Discovery of Lancaster/VH Dance (717-715-2448), Mulberry Art Studios, 21 North Mulberry Street, Lancaster.

Imani Edu-Tainers African Dance Company (717-808-0203), Mulberry Art Studios, 21 North Mulberry Street, Lancaster.

Lancaster School of Ballet (717-569-0955), 438 North Queen Street, Stahr Performing Arts center, Lancaster.

Viktor Yeliohin International Ballet Academy (717-517-9837), 214 West Grant Street, 2nd Floor, Lancaster.

World Dance Lancaster (717-951-5152), Mulberry Art Studios, 21 North Mulberry Street, Lancaster.

10 Special Events
WE'RE OPEN ALL YEAR LONG!

Most visitors come to Lancaster County during the summer months when school is out, the days are warm, and the all the stores and attractions are open. But prudent visitors will discover that Lancaster has a lot to share during other parts of the year, too. There are a host of annual festivals, celebrations, shows, exhibits, and tons of "just for fun" events to delight every member of the family—all year long. In fact, you might want to plan your own visit during one of the special events listed below and then build from there with the other sites listed in the previous nine chapters.

ALL YEAR

First Fridays. Downtown Lancaster celebrates the arts on the first Friday of every month. More than 70 different arts venues stay open late and offer special hospitality touches.

Music Fridays. Live outdoor music concerts (free) throughout downtown Lancaster on the third Friday of the month.

WINTER (DECEMBER-MARCH)

AQS Quilt Show and Contest (Lancaster; http://aqsshows.com/AQSLancaster). If you want to see some of the best contest quilts ever displayed then this is your show! Quilts from across the country and around the world are exhibited at this annual event.

Lititz Fire and Ice Festival (Lititz; www.lititzfireandicefestival.com). It's all here—a chili cook-off, Winter Wonderland Carnival, games, entertainment, family movie night, and a dodgeball tournament.

Lancaster County is quilt country.

SPRING (APRIL-MAY)

Annual Microfest (Adamstown; www.stoudtsbeer.com/events_micro-fest.html). Enjoy over 40 beers from America's finest breweries, great food and music. A ticket includes four hours of sampling, a buffet, live music, souvenir glass, and a free shuttle to and from select local hotels.

Antiques Capital U.S.A. Spring Extravaganza (Adamstown; www.antiquescapital.com/extrav.htm). Antique Extravaganza is a special event held three times per year (April, June, September). You'll find scores of antiques shops, including outdoor markets, thousands of dealers, and plenty of local lodging, restaurants and specialty shops in an area known among antiques aficionados as Antiques Capital USA.

Herb & Garden Faire (Landis Valley Museum, Lancaster; www.landisvalleymuseum.org). A great event for both gardeners and non-gardeners. Enjoy walking the grounds, shopping the stands of 80-plus vendors of herbs, perennials, annuals, natives, vegetables, and garden art.

Lancaster ArtWalk (Lancaster; http://lancasterartwalk.org). Held every May and September, this event celebrates the eclectic mix of independent galleries that thrives in downtown Lancaster. Take a contemplative walk with Lancaster's gallery community and enjoy meet-the-artist events, seminars, workshops, kids' activities and more.

Launch Music Festival (Lancaster; http://launchmusicconference.com). This annual late April event bills itself as follows: "175+ performers. 15 stages. 1 weekend. All styles of music."

Long's Park Art and Craft Festival (Lancaster; www.longspark.org/art .html). Experience one of America's top fine art and craft shows. For three days, Long's Park is transformed into an outdoor gallery. With 200 top artists and craftspeople from across the country, this annual event showcases the best artisans from throughout the U.S. Live music, fine food, wine and craft beer, too.

Rhubarb Festival (Kitchen Kettle Village; www.kitchenkettle.com/ events/rhubarb-festival.asp). Rhubarb is the harbinger of spring in Pennsylvania Dutch Country, and every year this celebration pays tribute with a two-day food festival filled with many delicious treats and an assortment of zany events.

Sertoma Club Annual Chicken Barbeque (Long's Park, Lancaster). If you're in town during the third week in May, then this is the place to be! Listed in the Guinness Book of World

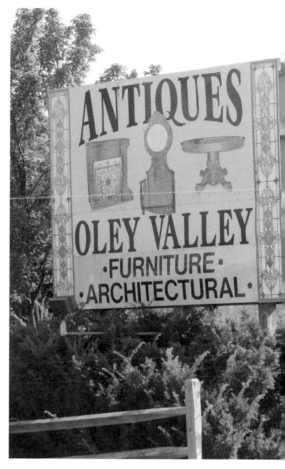

Adamstown is the antiques capital of the U.S.!

Records as the World's Largest Chicken Barbeque, this annual event will provide you with one of 33,000 chicken dinners for a donation of just $7. This is like a family reunion on steroids—thousands of your closest friends and loads of fun!

The Great Pennsylvania FlavorFest (Manheim; www.parenfaire.com/flavor fest). Held during Memorial Day weekend, the Great PA FlavorFest offers the best of Pennsylvania food, dining and entertainment. Twenty wineries provide complimentary samples of some of their most popular vintages, while food and craft vendors showcase their handmade delights.

Volksfest (Manheim; www.parenfaire.com/volksfest). If you love classic VWs, then come to Volksfest on the grounds of Mount Hope Estate. Check out the best

Long's Park Art and Craft Festival

of air- and water-cooled Volkswagens, and enjoy food from the Swashbuckler Grove Kitchens along with Swashbuckler Ales. Be sure to stay around for the large VW swap meet.

SUMMER (JUNE-AUGUST)

Annual Antique, Art & Craft Show (Columbia; www.parivertowns.com). This popular outdoor event held every June attracts over 200 vendors, who fill Locust Street Park and line the main thoroughfare. You'll find a mixture of crafts, antiques, food, and entertainment. (June)

Celebrate Lancaster (Lancaster; www.lancastercityevents.com/events/event-celebrate-lancaster.asp). This grand summer event brings over 15,000 people to downtown Lancaster to experience entertainment, food, and a fireworks display that can be seen throughout Lancaster County. The festival showcases the cultural and diversity of the people who live and work in Lancaster with local foods, locally crafted beer and wine, and professional, local and regional entertainment. (June)

Celtic Fling & Highland Games (Lebanon; www.parenfaire.com/celtic/main .php). The Celtic Fling & Highland Games celebrate all things Celtic. Enjoy traditional pipe bands, modern Celtic rock bands, and everything in between, plus delicious Celtic cuisine, fresh brewed Swashbuckler ales and more. (June)

Cherry Fair & Early American Craft Show (Schaefferstown). Held at the historic Alexander Schaeffer Farm, this annual show features quality period crafters, colonial demonstrations, family corner, hands-on activities, wagon rides, contests, guided house and heirloom garden tours, blacksmith shop and sawmill demos, raffles, sheep to shawl, cherry "goodies," tasty food, and homemade ice cream! (June)

Day Out with Thomas (Strasburg; www.strasburgrailroad.com/day-out with -thomas.php). Day Out with Thomas at the Strasburg Railroad is a family event that offers children and their parents the opportunity to ride with classic storybook friend Thomas the Tank Engine. Photo opportunities galore! (June, September, November)

Juneteenth Heritage Celebration (Lancaster; www.cacc-lancaster.org). Juneteenth is a celebration of the time when the last enslaved people finally learned that they were free in Galveston, Texas, nearly three years after the signing of the Emancipation Proclamation. This is a multicultural family event for sharing history through song, entertainment, and a special appearance by the Past Players of Pennsylvania. (June)

Lancaster Summer Arts Festival (Lancaster). A variety of day and evening events (all free) for children and adults. (June and July)

Long's Park Summer Music Series (Lancaster; www.longspark.org). Enjoy a variety of outdoor concerts by professional musicians every Sunday evening. (June through August)

Pennsylvania Renaissance Faire (Lebanon; www.parenaissancefaire.com). This medieval event begins on a weekend in August and lasts until October (weekends only). If you're looking to expose the family to knights in shining armor, people who eat swords, jousting exhibitions, interactive street performances, and fair damsels (not always in distress), then this is the place to check out.

The Pennsylvania Renaissance Faire

Stoudtburg Bavarian Village Arts & Crafts Festival (Adamstown; www .stoudtburgvillage.com). This festival is held in a quaint and charming model of a Bavarian village, complete with cobblestone streets, fountain, and old world Bavarian-style building architecture. The festival features arts-and-craft vendors specializing in unique handcrafted items. (June and October)

FALL (SEPTEMBER-NOVEMBER)

Annual Bridge Bust (Columbia; www.parivertowns.com/bridgebust.htm). If you've never been to a festival on a bridge that stretches 1.25 miles, then this is your chance! More than 300 vendors offer their wares in the categories of antiques, art, crafts, food, and unique items in this unique and popular event. The venue is the Route 462 Veterans Memorial Bridge between Columbia and Wrightsville.

Ephrata Fair (Ephrata; www.ephratafair.org). This annual event bills itself as the Largest Street Fair in Pennsylvania. The fair features a variety of agricultural events, parades, entertainment, live music, carnival rides, cookie-decorating contests, exhibits, and all the usual events associated with an all-encompassing people-packed festival.

The Annual Bridge Bust is held on the Wrightsville Bridge

Harvest Days at Landis Valley is a great family event.

Gift of Lights (Lititz; http://elizabeth farms.com/gift-of-lights). Treat the family to more than a mile of a drive-through display with hundreds of thousands of twinkling lights. Each year, more than 120,000 people visit this unique display.

Harvest Days at Landis Valley (Landis Valley; www.landisvalley museum.org). Here's an event for the whole family. Bring the kids for family-oriented demonstrations, exhibits, live music, horse-drawn wagon rides, and a children's discovery tent. Taste heritage varieties of apples and watch them get turned into cider or apple butter. Witness wool go from sheep to shawl, and enjoy all the plowing demonstrations.

Jason's Woods Haunted Attraction (Lancaster; www.jasonswoods.com). Weekends in October. If you're looking for a series of hair-raising experiences, cardiac arrests, and frightening adventures, then here you are. This is Halloween like you've never seen it before—the special effects and scream-filled attractions will leave you breathless.

Lancaster County Tailgating Festival (Kitchen Kettle Village; www.kitchen kettle.com/events/tailgating-festival.asp). Savor tasty samples of homemade tailgate foods, tap your toes to a Dixieland band, compete at the Pumpkin Whoopie Pie Filling Contest, jump in the bounce house, enter the tailgate toss, get your face painted, and watch the parade. Oh, don't forget my favorite event: pumpkin bowling!

Lititz Chocolate Walk (www.pavendors.com/events/lancaster-county/ lititz-pa-october-chocolate-walk.htm). The Lititz Chocolate Walk (every October) brings together some of the region's most talented chefs and candy makers. Get a button and a punch card and follow the maps through historic downtown Lititz, where chocolate treats are given out at each of the more than 20 stops. This event is often referred to as "trick-or-treat for grownups."

Long's Park Art & Craft Festival (Lancaster; www.longspark.org), 1441 Harrisburg Pike, Lancaster. Labor Day weekend. Experience one of America's top fine arts-and-crafts shows. For three days, shop and enjoy breathtaking creativity at a beautiful city park that has been transformed into an outdoor gallery with 200 top artists and craftspeople from across the country.

New Holland Farmers Fair (New Holland; http://newhollandfair.org). Funnel cake, sweet cinnamon rolls, and cotton candy are just some of the taste treats served up at this 75-year-old festival. There's also a midway, a parade, tractor-driving contest, a swine and sheep show, and a bake sale.

Oktoberfest (Lancaster; www.lancasterliederkranz.com/fests.html). This is Lancaster's oldest traditional Oktoberfest. Come join a celebration of German food, beer, song and dance. Wearing lederhosen is optional.

Snitz Fest (1719 Hans Herr House, Willow Street; www.hansherr.org/Home/

Chocolate is the theme at the annual Chocolate Walk

A stop on the Lititz Chocolate Walk

Events/Snitz_Fest). This popular annual Pennsylvania German festival—held on the grounds of the county's oldest home—features great food, interpreters in traditional dress, hands-on activities and demonstrations of Colonial-era arts, crafts and farm life: threshing, quilting, loom weaving, heckling flax, churning butter, cooking over a fire, and making shingles, shoes, candles, and cornhusk dolls.

Strictly Functional Pottery National (East Petersburg; www.strictly functionalpottery.net). This show will wow you with an amazing collection of some of the best pottery produced in the country. You have to see it to believe it.

Whoopie Pie Festival (Strasburg; http://whoopiepiefestival.com). Who can resist rich, creamy icing spread between two soft, delicious cakes? The annual event (in September) features more than 100 different whoopie pie flavors and is held at the Hershey Farm Restaurant & Inn.

MUD SALES

Mud Sale is the Lancaster County term for an annual auction and/or sale at a local fire company. Mud sales have helped build fire houses, purchase equipment, and enable training for firefighters. The sales, appropriately named for the condition of the thawing ground, attract thousands of people looking for bargains.

Items you're likely to discover at a mud sale include furniture, antiques, livestock, quilts, farm machinery, crafts, buggies, collectibles, barns, hay, woodcrafts, plants, tractors, and sporting goods.

Mud sales are scheduled throughout the year (rain or shine; mud or not). Most sales start early in the morning and last throughout the day. Be sure to come hungry because there will be plenty of food stands with all manner of goodies, including doughnuts, stromboli, barbecued chicken, sausage sandwiches, chicken corn noodle soup, soft pretzels, oyster sandwiches, smoked meats, cheeses, pies, cookies, breads, homemade ice cream, and more.

FEBRUARY

Strasburg Spring Consignment & Mud Sale (717-687-7232; http://strasburg fire.com/Events.aspx), Strasburg Fire Company #1, 203 Franklin St., Strasburg, PA 17579.

MARCH

Bart Township Annual Auction/Mud Sale (717-786-3348; www.bart51.com), Bart Twp. Fire Company, 11 Furnace Rd., Quarryville, PA 17566.

Gap Annual Spring Mud Sale/Auction (717-442-8100; www.gapfire.org), Gap Fire Company, 802 Pequea Ave., Gap, PA 17527.

Gordonville Spring Mud Sale & Auction (717-768-3869; www.gordon villefc.com), Gordonville Fire Company, Old Leacock Rd., Gordonville, PA 17529.

Penryn Fire Company Mud Sale (717-664-2825; www.penrynfire.com/ mudsale.htm), Penryn Fire Company #1, 1441 N. Penryn Rd., Manheim, PA 17545.

West Earl Mud Sale (717-656-6791; www.westearlfore.org), West Earl Fire Company, 14 School Lane Ave., Brownstown, PA 17508.

APRIL

Rawlinsville Annual Mud Sale (717-284-3023; www.rvfd58.com), Rawlins-ville Fire Company, 33 Martic Heights Dr., Holtwood, PA 17532.

Come to the Whoopie Pie Festival at Hershey Farm

The Strasburg Fire Company has a mud sale every February

Robert Fulton Volunteer Fire Company Mud Sale (717-548-8995; www.513 rffc.com), Robert Fulton Fire Company, 2271 Robert Fulton Hwy., Peach Bottom, PA 17563.

MAY

Gratz Area Fire Company Annual Consignment Sale (717-365-3043; www .gratzfirecompanysale.com), Gratz Fairgrounds, 601 East Market St. (Rt. 25), Gratz, PA 17030.

Honeybrook Annual Auction/Mud Sale (610-273-2688; www.honeybrookfire .org), Honeybrook Fire Company, 679 Firehouse Lane, Honeybrook, PA 19344.

JUNE

Bird-in-Hand Mud Sale | Lancaster County Carriage & Antique Auction (717-392-0112), Along Rt. 340 (Old Philadelphia Pike) across from Bird-in-Hand Family Restaurant, Bird-in-Hand, PA.

Refton Fire Company Sale (717-786-9462; www.refton59fire.org), Refton Fire Company, 99 Church Street, Refton, PA 17568.

AUGUST

Bareville Fire Company Mud Sale (717-656-7554; www.barevillefire.com), Bareville Volunteer Fire Company, 211 East Main St., Leola, PA 17540.

Kinzer Fire Company Mud Sale (717-442-9148; www.kinzerfire.com), Kinzer Fire Company, 3521 Lincoln Highway East, Kinzers, PA 17535.

OCTOBER

Cochranville Fire Company Mud Sale (610-593-5800; www.cochranvillefire .com), Cochranville Volunteer Fire Company, 3135 Limestone Rd., Cochranville, PA 19330.

Information is readily available wherever you travel

11 Information, Please
IN THE KNOW

Representatives of Lancaster and Lancaster County go out of their way to make sure visitors are provided with the most up-to-date information about every possible tourist attraction, site, or destination possible. This is truly a visitor-friendly county—one where folks will stop to give you directions, volunteers will cheerfully guide you through a historical exhibit, and multiple visitors' centers will provide you with every possible brochure that has ever been printed.

To put it mildly, you will not lack for information, either prior to your visit or anytime during your visit. In fact, you may need an extra suitcase just to transport all the printed information back home. Whether your visit is for a day, a week, or something much longer you will discover that there are scores of folks eager to help you learn about this dynamic region in addition to assisting you in getting to each place on your itinerary.

Take advantage of all the resources listed in this chapter. Fill up on information guides and Internet sites. Be sure to take some time to talk with the always-friendly folks at each place you visit. They are a major part of the reason why Lancaster County is a favorite of folks from across the street or around the world.

INFORMATION CENTERS IN LANCASTER COUNTY

Downtown Lancaster Visitors Center (717-735-0823; www.padutchcountry .com), Heritage Center Penn Square, 5 West King St., Lancaster, PA 17603. Adjacent to Central Market, this informative center will provide you with the usual array of brochures and guides with a particular emphasis on things to do in the city of Lancaster. Lots of great resources.

Lititz Springs Park Welcome Center

Elizabethtown Area Chamber of Commerce (717-361-7188; www.elizabeth towncoc.com), 50 South Wilson Ave., Elizabethtown, PA 17022. Get the most up-to-date information about the Elizabethtown area from these fine folks.

Ephrata Area Information Center (717-738-9010; www.ephrata-area.org), 16 East Main St., Ephrata, PA 17522. The Ephrata area and surrounding communities are nestled in the rich farmland that is home to the Pennsylvania Dutch. Begin your journey throughout Ephrata here.

> **F**AST FACT: Members of the Ephrata Cloister were required to sleep on wooden benches 15 inches wide, with wooden blocks for pillows.

Lititz Springs Park Welcome Center (717-626-8981; www.lititzsprings park.org/lspwelcome.html), 18 North Broad St., Lititz, PA 17543. Housed in a replica of an old train station, this is the place to come for all the information and guidance needed for a complete tour of Lititz and the surrounding area.

Manheim Visitors Center (717-665-1762; www.manheimdowntown .com), 17 North Main St., Manheim, PA 17545. Filled with historic architecture, culture, and a unique sprit, Manheim is a must-stop on your journeys through Lancaster County. This center has everything you need.

> **F**AST FACT: There are nearly 2 million Mennonites around the world, in countries as diverse as India, Ethiopia, Canada, Tanzania, Germany, Paraguay, and Mexico. New York City is home to more than 20 Mennonite congregations.

Mennonite Information Center (717-299-0954;www.mennoniteinfoctr.com/), 2209 Millstream Rd., Lancaster, PA 17602. Chock full of books, magazines, brochures, and pamphlets about the Amish and Mennonites, this place has some of the friendliest folks in town. Get all your questions answered and find everything you're looking for in this delightful center.

Mount Joy Chamber of Commerce and Visitors Center (717-653-0773; www .mountjoychamber.com), 62 East Main Street, Mount Joy, PA 17552. Information on things to do and places to see can be obtained in this informative hub.

Pennsylvania Dutch Country Visitor's Center

Pennsylvania Dutch Country Visitors Center (800-723-8824; www.padutch country.com), 501 Greenfield Rd., Lancaster, PA 17601. One of two official visitor information centers (Downtown Lancaster Visitors Center, mentioned previously, is the other), this is the "granddaddy" of all visitor centers. Offering brochures, information, guides, flyers, books, a free film, and creative visual displays this is the place to come for information. The always-friendly and always-courteous folks here will guide, direct, instruct, inform and enlighten you about all the sights of Lancaster County. The Center should definitely be your first stop on any visit to Lancaster County.

Susquehanna Valley Chamber of Commerce and Visitors Center (717-684-5249; www.parivertowns.com), 445 Linden Street, Columbia, PA 17512. If you're looking for things to do and places to visit in western Lancaster County, then this is the place. The focus is on the three river towns of Marietta, Columbia, and Wrightsville.

FOLLOW LANCASTER COUNTY

You can keep up with all the latest happenings in Lancaster County through the following social media sites:

Facebook: facebook.com/golancasterpa
Flickr: flickr.com/golancasterpa
Twitter: twitter.com/golancasterpa
YouTube: youtube.com/golancaster

THE LANCASTER COUNTY EXPLORATION GUIDE

The Lancaster County Exploration Guide app (www.PaDutchCountry.com/app) has a number of features that can help make your visit to Lancaster County complete. Included on this *free* app are:

❖ A complete calendar with information about what's happening at any time of the year.

❖ An interactive map that will pinpoint your present location and all the attractions located in the immediate vicinity.

❖ A selection of sample itineraries that offer the entire family an array of things to do and places to see.

❖ Coupons and special offers.

❖ A direct line to the Lancaster County Visitors Center information desk.

Homemade root beer is the best!

APPENDIX:
FAVORITE LANCASTER COUNTY RECIPES

Yum! If there is one thing that distinguishes Lancaster County from other counties, it's the food. Everywhere you travel throughout Lancaster, you are sure to come upon some food-related enterprise along the road. These may include all-you-can-eat smorgasbords, family bakeries specializing in some sweet and sinful treats, European-style restaurants, one-of-a-kind cafés, or farmer's markets with an array of food items that would put most urban supermarkets to shame. In short, this is the land of victuals, rations, and cuisine . . . and the never-ending celebration of that food.

The following recipes, collected from throughout the county, offer you and your family several delicious reminders of your visit to Lancaster County. Share these treats with guests and friends and perhaps they too will want to take a memorable journey to Lancaster County.

CHICKEN CORN SOUP

One of the classic Lancaster County dishes is chicken corn soup. This is a great winter-time dinner or a tasty midday meal. Add some homemade biscuits with strawberry jam, and you'll have a meal the family will demand with increasing regularity. This old family recipe is direct from a Lancaster County farm:

4 cups water
1½ teaspoons salt
3½ pounds stewing chicken (with bones)
1 chicken bouillon cube
1½ pints fresh or frozen corn
½ cup chopped celery
1 small onion (chopped)
½ cup broken noodles
2 hard-boiled eggs (chopped)
salt & pepper

Put the water in a large pot and add the salt. Place the chicken in the pot and boil until the chicken is tender. Remove the chicken and cut it into small pieces. Add the bouillon cube to the broth along with the chicken, corn, celery, onion, and noodles. Bring to a boil and then turn the heat down to low. Cook for about 30 minutes and then ladle into bowls. Sprinkle the chopped eggs into each bowl. Use salt and pepper to taste.

NOTE: You may wish to adjust the amount of water depending on whether you want a thicker or thinner soup.

SHOO-FLY PIE (MAKES TWO 8-INCH PIES)

One of the "basic" food items throughout the Amish countryside is shoo-fly pie. Although there is no consensus on this matter, it is believed that this calorie-rich dessert got its name from the fact that it was made with *very* sweet ingredients that tended to attract lots of flies. When you have lots of flies in your kitchen, you need to "shoo" them away—thus the name.

You can find shoo-fly pie at almost every farm stand, grocery store, and restaurant throughout Lancaster County. Or you can create your own shoo-fly pie at home with this very simple recipe:

CRUMB TOPPING

¾ cup brown sugar
⅓ cup solid shortening
2 cups flour

FILLING

1 cup very thick molasses (use good-quality molasses)
½ cup brown sugar
2 beaten eggs
1 teaspoon baking soda
1 cup boiling water

CRUST

two 8-inch unbaked pie shells

Preheat your oven to 400°. In a medium-size bowl mix together all three ingredients for the crumb topping (it may be lumpy). Set aside. In another bowl, combine the molasses, ½ cup of brown sugar and the eggs. Dissolve the baking

Satisfy your sweet tooth with shoo-fly pie.

soda in the boiling water and add to the syrup mixture. Mix completely until all ingredients are thoroughly combined. Pour some of the syrup mixture into each of the pie shells. Sprinkle with some of the crumbs and then pour on the rest of the syrup. Cover the top of each pie with the remainder of the crumb mixture. Bake at 400° for 10 minutes. Reduce the heat to 350° and bake for an additional 50 minutes. Serve the pie warm.

LANCASTER COUNTY PRETZELS

Pretzels are one of the staple foods of Lancaster County. Sometime during your journeys you may have visited a pretzel factory or taken the opportunity to make your own pretzels. The following recipe is a classic, and it's fun for the entire family—turn the kitchen into your own pretzel factory! One warning: Once you taste these delicious treats, you may never go back to store-bought pretzels again.

PRETZELS

2 teaspoons active yeast
½ cup plus 1 cup warm water
1 tablespoon sugar
1 teaspoon salt
4 cups bread flour
1 cup water (room temperature)
butter for coating the dough

SODA SOLUTION

4 cups boiling water
3 teaspoons baking soda

Dissolve the yeast in ½ cup of warm water. When dissolved, stir in an additional cup of water. Add the sugar and salt and mix thoroughly. Pour this mixture into a large bowl and beat in the bread flour until you have a stiff dough. Turn out the dough onto a floured surface and knead for a few minutes. Put the dough into a greased bowl. Spread the surface of the dough with butter. Cover the bowl with a cloth and set it in a warm location. Allow the dough to rise until it doubles in size.

Put 4 cups of water into a large pot and bring to a boil. Add 3 teaspoons of baking soda and stir thoroughly. Set aside.

Remove the dough from the bowl and form into pretzels about as thick as your little finger. Pinch the ends of the pretzels tight onto the main loop. (You may want to have some commercial pretzels on hand to use as models.) Dip each pretzel into the soda water until it floats. Remove the pretzels and allow them to drain. Sprinkle each with salt. (Pretzel salt is best. You can obtain this online or at many large grocery stores. Great American Spice Company and Morton Salt are two companies that make pretzel salt.)

Place the pretzels on a greased cookie sheet and bake at 475° for about 12 minutes or until they are a golden brown. Serve warm. For a real Pennsylvania treat, dip your warm pretzels in yellow mustard and enjoy.

AMISH CHOW CHOW

Chow chow is a way of preserving a bounty of vegetables to enjoy all year long. While the name of this Lancaster County treat may seem unusual, your family will discover that the taste is not. Chow chow can be paired with almost everything, especially in the winter months. The combination of tastes will have your family begging you to make more.

1 cup chopped green tomatoes

1 cup chopped bell peppers

1 whole cucumber, chopped

1 cup chopped onions

2 quarts water

¼ cup salt

1 cup chopped carrots

1 cup chopped green beans

1 cup chopped cabbage

2 teaspoons mustard seed

2 teaspoons celery seed

2 cups cider vinegar

2 cups sugar

Chow Chow is good good!

Soak the tomatoes, peppers, cucumber, and onions overnight in salted water. Drain. Cook the carrots and green beans for 10 minutes and drain. Mix all the ingredients together in a large pot. Heat to a boil. Pack in sterile jars and seal.

AMISH ROOT BEER

You've probably had several different brands of commercial root beer, but you've probably never had homemade root beer. Travel around Lancaster County long enough and you'll discover numerous handmade signs advertising homemade Root Beer. A frosty glassful on a hot summer's day is truly a treat for the palate and the senses. Now you can make your own right at home. Just watch the smiles spread across everyone's faces.

1 teaspoon yeast
1½ cups sugar
4 teaspoons root beer extract (McCormick and Zatarain's are brands to look for)
Warm water

Dissolve the yeast in one cup of warm water and place in a gallon jar. Add the sugar and root beer extract with enough warm water to dissolve thoroughly. Stir until everything is completely dissolved. Fill the remainder of the jar with warm water and set the jar out in the sun or on a warm windowsill. Allow the jar to sit for several hours or until the mixture is strong enough for your taste. Place the jar in the refrigerator until chilled. Serve and enjoy.

INDEX